Our Debt to Greece and Rome

EDITORS
George Depue Hadzsits, Ph.D.
University of Pennsylvania

David Moore Robinson, Ph.D., LL.D.
The Johns Hopkins University

CONTRIBUTORS TO THE "OUR DEBT TO GREECE AND ROME FUND," WHOSE GENEROSITY HAS MADE POSSIBLE THE LIBRARY

Our Debt to Greece and Rome

Philadelphia
Dr. Astley P. C. Ashhurst
John C. Bell
Henry H. Bonnell
Jasper Yeates Brinton
John Cadwalader
Miss Clara Comegys
Miss Mary E. Converse
Arthur G. Dickson
William M. Elkins
William P. Gest
John Gribbel
Samuel F. Houston
John Story Jenks
Alba B. Johnson
Miss Nina Lea
George McFadden
Mrs. John Markoe
Jules E. Mastbaum
J. Vaughan Merrick
Effingham B. Morris
William R. Murphy
John S. Newbold
S. Davis Page (*memorial*)
Owen J. Roberts
Joseph G. Rosengarten
John B. Stetson, Jr.
Dr. J. William White (*memorial*)
Owen Wister
The Philadelphia Society for the Promotion of Liberal Studies.

Boston
Oric Bates (*memorial*)
Frederick P. Fish
William Amory Gardner
Joseph Clark Hoppin

Chicago
Herbert W. Wolff

Cincinnati
Charles Phelps Taft

Detroit
John W. Anderson
Dexter M. Ferry, Jr.

Doylestown, Pennsylvania
"A Lover of Greece and Rome"

New York
John Jay Chapman
Willard V. King
Thomas W. Lamont
Elihu Root
Mortimer L. Schiff
William Sloane
George W. Wickersham
And one contributor, who has asked to have his name withheld:
Maecenas atavis edite regibus, O et praesidium et dulce decus meum.

Washington
The Greek Embassy at Washington, for the Greek Government.

RELIEF IN CONSTANTINOPLE

Representing the seated Euripides receiving the tragic mask from *Skene*. The statue of Dionysus, the patron-god of tragedy, is behind Euripides.

EURIPIDES AND HIS INFLUENCE

BY
F. L. LUCAS, M.A.
Fellow of King's College, Cambridge

INTRODUCTION BY
R. W. LIVINGSTONE

MARSHALL JONES COMPANY
BOSTON · MASSACHUSETTS

COPYRIGHT·1923·BY MARSHALL JONES COMPANY

All rights reserved

Printed October, 1923

THE PLIMPTON PRESS·NORWOOD·MASSACHUSETTS
PRINTED IN THE UNITED STATES OF AMERICA

To

MY WIFE

INTRODUCTION

THERE are many signs that the present generation will see what Europe has seen twice in the last five hundred years—a Greek Renaissance. Ever since Greek letters after a long night became part of the common heritage of Europe, Greek literature has had its worshippers, and in each century individuals have penetrated behind the literary beauty to the living soul of Greece. Schoolmasters like Ascham, politicians like Charles James Fox, no less than poets like Milton and Shelley, have made the discovery, drawn by some inner kinship of spirit, or finding their way by accident or instinct to sources where the needs of their nature could be satisfied. What happens to individuals in every age happens more rarely to Europe itself. There are two fountains of living waters, to which human nature turns when the sky is as brass above and the earth as iron beneath. One of them springs from Greek soil; and from

INTRODUCTION

time to time ages as well as individuals have recourse to it, not for mere literary enjoyment but for an ideal of life. There are many signs of such a movement to-day. This book and the series in which it appears are among them.

Euripides has been the centre of the awakened interest in Greece. That is partly because he has found in this generation a translator and an interpreter of genius: partly because the twentieth century sees in him its own critical spirit, its hatred of cruelty and religious shams, its sympathy with women and with the oppressed. Indeed he has sometimes been regarded almost as the private property of an age when these feelings have been more common and perhaps less impotent than is usual in human history. Mr. Lucas, already known among the younger generation of scholars for his gifts of style and literary criticism, deals in this book chiefly with the influence of Euripides throughout the ages, and incidentally correct such exclusiveness; for he shows that Euripides has had his followers in every age and that of all the Greek dramatists he has most continually moved the hearts of men.

His book has thus a double interest. It supplies materials and guidance for a purely liter-

INTRODUCTION

ary study. It shows what writers fell under the spell of Euripides; who ignored or were repelled by him; what qualities in him attracted this man or that, one age or another; what poets as different as Virgil, Milton and Racine owed to the Greek; how different epochs understood or misunderstood him; how his successive creditors borrowed and used their borrowings. It raises the whole question of literary imitation and literary inspiration, their nature, methods and limits. All this is a fascinating study in literary criticism. But it carries with it something more. It has a human interest of its own, for it is a study in the psychology of many men and diverse ages, and it gives some answer to the question, what is permanent in literature, what is transitory; what flames blaze brightly in their own generation and are extinct in the next, what lights, once lit, burn for ever.

R. W. LIVINGSTONE
Fellow of Corpus Christi, Oxford

PREFACE

> "Our souls are like those orphans whose unwedded mothers died in bearing them; the secret of our paternity lies in their graves and we must go there to learn it."
> HERMAN MELVILLE

"IT is said," writes Gibbon, "that the foolish curiosity of Elagabalus attempted to discover from the quantity of spider-webs the number of the inhabitants of Rome." It is not, perhaps, really a much wiser curiosity that hopes to determine by raking in the cobwebs of libraries the undying influence of one dead mind on a hundred subsequent generations. In each of them only a tiny minority has written books that endure; from a criticism here, an imitation there, we have to divine what Euripides meant to the writers and to their voiceless contemporaries,—to the spirit of a whole era. When we speak of the influence of Euripides, we are concerned not only with its obvious manifestations, those revivals and *remaniements* of which even this jaded age is not yet weary (as I write, the *Alcestis* has

PREFACE

just been performed in that stronghold of the Middle Ages, the Glastonbury of Arthur and Joseph of Arimathea, and *Medea* is appearing on the London stage); his tradition lives on in far other, subtler ways as well. The seamen of the Napoleonic Wars who miscalled their ship the "Billy Ruffian" or those who in the last great struggle manned the "Niffie Jane," knew nothing of the author of *Bellerophon* and *Iphigenia*, but here too, ultimately, is the influence of Euripides. The working of a great spirit is a silent, subtle thing—"closer is He than breathing and nearer than hands and feet." With the passing of the years it becomes an imperceptible part of the intellectual atmosphere of the world; as the fine dust of a bursting volcano at the Antipodes has, weeks after, kindled to unwonted splendour the sunsets of another hemisphere. Chapter and verse citations of allusions and borrowings can give only a fragmentary record of such an influence; and even that fragment is apt to be garbled by critics hungry for striking results. An Emil Reich will "explain" that wild adventure, the French Revolution, by the influence in the nurseries of France of a newly translated *Robinson Crusoe;* a Churton Collins by

PREFACE

a tireless accumulation of parallel platitudes will detect in Shakespeare the influence of almost every Greek poet extant. I can promise no such fireworks; and all that can here be attempted is some account of the effect on a number of playwrights and some thinkers and famous men of Euripides the Dramatist and Poet-Philosopher. For in this double aspect antiquity always saw him, honouring alike the creator and the critic of life; whereas the seventeenth and eighteenth centuries thought of him, for better or worse, purely as a playwright; and now the late nineteenth and the twentieth, disgorging tome after tome on the Ideas of Euripides, seem in some danger of forgetting that he was after all dramatist, not pamphleteer. It is mainly with his influence on the drama, the most Greek of all our arts—Greek indeed down to its very terminology, "tragedy" and "comedy," "prologue" and "epilogue," "orchestra" and "scene"—that we shall be concerned; yet not forgetting that, quite outside the stage-door, there lies a different interest, deeper than can attach to dreary lists of poetasters who have botched up his plays and of criticasters who have pulled them to pieces—the interest of following from age to

PREFACE

age across the lips of men as diverse as Alexander and Clement of Alexandria, Caesar and Brutus, Cicero and St. Paul, Milton and Goethe, Cardinal Newman and Bernard Shaw, the echoes of this Euripides, who has so long out-lived his own theatre, his own tongue, his own gods, as, it may be, he will outlast ours. The roll of his past lovers can be no barren study for those who love him still.

*"Perhaps this very woodland here
Is lovelier than it used to be,
Because some other held it dear
    And stood and looked from tree to tree
    And loved it long ago."*

CONTENTS

CHAPTER	PAGE
Contributors to the Fund	ii
Introduction *by R. W. Livingstone*	vii
Preface	xi
I. The Man and His Work	3
II. The Influence of Euripides on Antiquity	39
III. Middle Ages and Renaissance	82
IV. The Neo-Classic Age	118
V. The Nineteenth Century and After	152
Notes	179
Bibliography	186

EURIPIDES
AND HIS INFLUENCE

EURIPIDES AND HIS INFLUENCE

I. THE MAN AND HIS WORK

> "I know not if I deserve that a laurel-wreath should one day be laid on my coffin.... But lay on my coffin a sword; for I was a brave soldier in the war of liberation of humanity."
>
> HEINE

THE life of the most tragic of the Attic dramatists coincides with a strange exactness with the dawn and noon and twilight of his city's splendour. For he was born, says tradition, in the very years, nay on the very day, of the battle at Salamis,[1] the beginning of her supremacy in Hellas; his prime saw her an imperial city, with Pericles at her head and the Parthenon rising on Athena's Hill; and a timely death alone spared his old age the last defeat at Ægospotami, the agony of the siege, the breaking of the Long Walls and of the empire of Athens.

EURIPIDES AND HIS INFLUENCE

The parentage of Euripides was the inexhaustible jest of the Comic Poets; yet his mother, described by them as a greengrocer whose very greens were bad, seems really to have been of gentle birth, while his father was at least comfortably middle-class. The latter, misled by a prophecy that the lad would gain victories hereafter, is said to have had him trained at first as an athlete, not without success; so that personal experience may lie behind the bitter aphorism in one of the plays, that "of all the million plagues of Hellas there is none worse than the race of athletes."[2] Next he tried his hand at painting; and he must have served too in army or fleet, since in his twenty-first year (459 B.C.) Athens found herself at bay both to east and west, and an ancient stone still records the death of her sons on six fronts in that one year.

But more momentous in the young poet's life was the gathering in Athens of the thinkers of all Greece, men like Anaxagoras (who came in 462), Protagoras, and Prodicus; certainly the first influenced him strongly; and the same dauntless intellectualism, the same arraignment of all things in Heaven and earth, that brought to each of them both fame and persecution in

Hellas, was to be at once the strength and the weakness, the making and the undoing, of the plays of the "Philosopher of the Stage" and friend of Socrates.

In 455, the year of the death of Æschylus, Euripides produced his first trilogy,—the beginning of half a century of continuous production, which was rewarded with repeated defeats at the hands of long forgotten rivals and only five victories, the last one after his death. It is, however, to the second half of this period, the last twenty-five years of the poet's life, that all the extant plays belong, except the *Alcestis*, the story of the egoist who let his wife die for him, and perhaps the *Cyclops*, a burlesque on the blinding of Polyphemus by Odysseus. Through all that gloomy quarter of a century Athens stood at bay in the struggle that was to prove her ruin; and under the nightmare of the plague, the tyranny of war-mad demagogues, the shame of defeats and, still worse, of victories savagely abused, her spirit sank and soured. And through it wrote the old Euripides, loathing alike the cold militarism of Sparta and the red imperialism of Athens, disliked and suspected by his countrymen, baited by the Comic Poets.

Once he was indicted for impiety; always he maintained an aloofness, eccentric in Athenian eyes, from public life—an unsociable hermit, lurking now in his library, the first ever formed in Athens, now in his study, a sea-cave on the isle of Salamis.

Such was the atmosphere in which the bulk of our plays found birth—the *Medea* (431 B.C.), the tragedy of Woman against Man and East against West, of the revenge that feeds on its own flesh; the *Hecuba,* another tragedy of Greek oppression and Oriental vengeance; the *Hippolytus* (428), Greek counterpart of the tale of Potiphar's wife; the *Heracles Mad,* tale of divine injustice and human loyalty; the *Ion,* the most anti-religious, and the *Trojan Women* (415), the most anti-imperialist, of all the plays; the *Electra* (413), one more denunciation of the blindness of vengeance and vendetta; the *Iphigenia in Tauris* with its escape into romance; and some half-dozen more.

Then suddenly in 408 the old poet, now over seventy, accepted an invitation to the Court of Macedon and shook the dust of Athens from his feet; it is as if the yearning of his choruses to fly away and be at rest had found at last fulfilment. There, with his genius seeming to find its youth again among the wild northern hills, he wrote his two most vividly romantic works, *The Bacchants* and the *Iphigenia at Aulis;* and there, torn to pieces by the royal hunting-pack like his own Pentheus, says the dubious legend, he died, and, though Athens asked vainly to be allowed to build the tomb of her dead prophet, he was entombed in Macedon.

Before discussing their influence, it will be necessary to outline the salient characteristics of the plays themselves.

First then come those innovations of Euripides in technique which have left their mark on the drama to this day. Tragedy had commenced with the ritual dances of a chorus of rustics; the change from Dance to Drama, from Religion to Art, began only when Thespis introduced the first actor, who during the intervals between dances "in turn playing many parts"—hero, tyrant, messenger, ghost, and god—could both declaim in monologue to the audience and make dialogue with the leader of the Chorus. From the moment of its admission the dramatic element grows at the expense of the lyric; Æschylus adds a second actor, Sophocles a third. Still in Sophocles, although the Chorus has been degraded from protagonist to spectator, their songs remain an integral part of the play; it is Euripides, with so much more modernity in his atmosphere, so much more intrigue in his plots, who becomes really embarrassed by this religious relic, this standing stage-army; so that his Chorus tends to fade into the background and become a choir of beautiful, but ineffectual angels, and their songs, lovely as they are, to grow more irrelevant, more like the musical overtures between the acts of a modern play. The characters of Æschylus are demigods, his choruses men; the characters of Euripides are men, his choruses ghosts. True, their irrelevance has been exaggerated,—Echo may vanish to a mere voice in the air, yet still answer to reality, and his lyrics will almost always be found relevant to the feeling, if not to the action, of the scenes they link together; still this weakness was already recognized and condemned by Aristotle.[3] Yet the change was doubly inevitable; for music was developing as well as drama, and Euripides who as a great musician could bind his own age with a double spell that is lost for us, introduced more and more singing by individual actors at the expense of the Chorus,—a still closer anticipation of modern opera. At the same time in all singing, as old-fashioned writers of the period complain, the new music was beginning to degrade the actual words to the unimportance of the modern libretto. Thus Euripides brings us half way from the ancient sense of orchestra, "dancing-place of the Chorus," to the modern; and his Chorus in its divorce from the action already anticipates its Senecan and Renaissance counterpart, limited to giving recitations between the Acts,—the last phase before its total extinction. The gaps left by its disappearance are the intervals between the Acts of the modern play, whose structure is thus the legacy of Greece by way of Seneca. Greek Tragedy had begun with dialogue as a relief to its Choric song; it ends with song as a relief to its dialogue.

A second far-reaching innovation of Euripides is the Prologue. The Greek term signified merely "that part of the play before the entrance of the Chorus"; and he is the originator of the thing in its modern sense of an introductory monologue addressed directly to the audience. Greek Tragedy was restricted for its plots to the legends of the Heroic Age, and, large as this cycle was, the audience must generally have known the story of the play. As Dryden says, "the people, as soon as they heard the name of Œdipus, knew as well as the poet that he had killed his father by a mistake, and committed incest with his mother, before the play; that they were now to hear of a great plague, an oracle, and the ghost of Laius: so that they sat with a yawning kind of expectation, till he was to come with his eyes pulled out, and speak a hundred or two verses in a tragic tone, in complaint of his misfortune." [4] All this being true (except the ghost, who belongs to Seneca, and the yawns which do not belong to Sophocles), the usual sort of exposition employed by Sophocles and Æschylus, who expect the audience to pick up the thread without much direct explanation, ought, one would think, to have been quite adequate, even in the absence of printed programmes. Euripides, however, whether from his passion for intellectual clearness and for throwing all his cards on the table at once, or out of consideration for the less literate among his hearers, made a practice of opening his plays by a monologue fired pointblank at the audience, which gives a summary, often extremely prosy, of previous events, and, if a god or ghost is the speaker, of the future course of the plot as well. For him, as for Boileau, "Le sujet n'est jamais assez tôt expliqué." *Iphigenia in Tauris* begins with a neat "Who's Who" of her family. Hermes predicts, not quite with divine accuracy, the *dénouement* of the *Ion*. This device, ridiculed by Aristophanes for its monotony, was transmitted by Seneca to the Renaissance; and the ghost-prologue of the *Hecuba,* twice copied by the Roman, became so ludicrously popular, that the correct Renaissance playwright felt it almost a point of honour to commence with some gibbering phantom:

*"Then too a filthy, whining ghost,
Lapt in some foul sheet or a leather pilch,
Comes screaming like a pig half-stickt
And cries 'Vindicta—Revenge, revenge!'"* [5]

Thus Milton himself planned a play about Macbeth to begin with Duncan's ghost.

A similar, though less obvious claim may be made for the Euripidean origin of the Epilogue, based not only on the tag of comment on life's uncertainty or of prayer for the poet's victory with which the Chorus closes a number of the plays, but also on his use of the *deus ex machina*. His fondness for this device is a much misunderstood commonplace. He did not invent it; the final epiphany of a divine figure may well have been an integral part of the original ritual dance; certainly it occurred in lost plays of Æschylus. Nor again is the god in the machine brought in just to cut a knot too hard for the dramatist to untie,—a fallacy perpetuated by Horace. The Imperial official in Chinese drama, the Royal officer in Molière's *Tartuffe*, who put everybody and everything in their right places at the close, are examples of the *deus ex machina* in the popular sense; but Athena, for instance, in the *Iphigenia in Tauris* is so far from being dragged in to straighten out the plot, that the plot is specially reknotted to bring her in. She speaks what is simply an epilogue revealing the future fortunes of hero and heroine, much as Scott does at the end of a novel, thus fitting the story the poet has used, back into the known legend-cycle. True, Euripides makes his traditional heroes so unconventionally human that sometimes nothing less than a god can bring them to their traditional ends; but in such cases the drama is really over before the god appears. In Euripides the *deus ex machina* is really an epilogue.

Of more interest is the advance made by him towards a greater complication of plot, a more careful development of suspense and surprise, as for instance in the melodramatic vicissitudes of the *Orestes* and the *Ion*. The latter with its recognition of a lost infant by its trinkets is the obvious parent of all those Fourth Century and Roman Comedy plots with their quiverfuls of missing offspring identified at the crucial moment, and a more distant ancestor of the long-lost heirs with strawberry-marks, of modern melodrama.

But more epoch-making still is the entrance of Love on the stage of Euripides. The buoyant romance of the lost *Andromeda,* with its rescue of the heroine from the sea-monster at dawn by the young hero, to whom she cries with a strange anticipation of the very words of Miranda to Ferdinand in *The Tempest,* "Take me, O stranger, as thou wilt, for maid or bride or slave of thine,"[6] the jealousy of Medea, the dark, unhappy loves of Phaedra and Stheneboea, the perverse passions of

Canace and Pasiphae—all these were treatments of a theme which, hackneyed to-day, was then a fiercely criticized innovation on the stage. "None knows of a woman in love in any play of mine" is the boast of Æschylus in the *Frogs* of Aristophanes, as he denounces Euripides on this very ground; but since Euripides there has lived not one great dramatist who could make the same disclaimer.

But though here the younger rival has set the fashion once for all, another side of his originality lay unrevived for over two thousand years, and the writer of the first *drames à thèse,* the first discussion-plays, lacked a successor, with the dramatically unsatisfactory exception of Voltaire, till the nineteenth century brought Ibsen and Dumas. In his introduction to Brieux, with his usual mixture of horse-sense and *enfant terrible,* Shaw writes: "The reason why Shakespeare and Molière are always well spoken of and recommended to the young, is that their quarrel is really a quarrel with God for not making men better. If they had quarreled with a specified class of persons with incomes of four figures for not doing their work better, or for doing no work at all, they would be denounced as seditious, impious,

THE MAN AND HIS WORK

and profligate corruptors of morality." Euripides conducted the first quarrel, as well as the second, to the bitter end; but Shaw's words well describe both the new poet's contrast with his predecessors and his unpopularity with his contemporaries. Life at large all great literature, not to say drama, must of its nature criticize; but the use of the theatre to defy the conventions and taboos of an age, to challenge the conscience of a people—as Nathan, David's, or Hamlet, the King's—was a new thing when Euripides braved twenty thousand of his countrymen in the theatre of Dionysus with plays where the shams of priestcraft and statecraft and conquest were stripped bare, and the despised woman or barbarian or slave put to shame the complacent pride of the Athenian *Bourgeoisie*. Not Ibsen, not Voltaire, not Tolstoi ever forged a keener weapon in defence of womanhood, in defiance of superstition, in denunciation of war, than the *Medea*, the *Ion*, the *Trojan Women*. Take the climax of Medea's vindication of her sex:

*"Men say we women lead a sheltered life
At home, while they face death amid the spears.*

*The fools! I had rather stand in the battle line
Thrice, than once bear a child."* [7]

Is there anything like it in literature till we come to the *Doll's House?*—

TORVALD: No man ever sacrifices his honour, even for one he loves.
NORA: Millions of women have done so.

Again, any thinking spectator must have felt —as he was meant to feel—towards Apollo in the *Ion* or Dionysus in *The Bacchants,* exactly like the man in Plutarch's story, who when he heard chanted in the theatre the praises of the savage Artemis, broke in upon the singer with the angry cry: "I wish you just such another daughter for your own!" [8] Euripides assails the Olympians from the very altar of Dionysus with the legends that were once made for their glory. And as a last instance of this freedom of utterance as well as thought, let suffice the challenge of the *Trojan Women* of 415 to the proud Demos of Athens, who the year before had massacred all the men in the little isle of Melos and sold their women and children as slaves, who in this very year were sending forth their great, doomed armada to conquer Sicily:

"*O fools, that sack the citied homes of men*
And waste their temples and the tombs, where sleep
The sacred dead,—then pass to death themselves!" [9]

Falstaff may question the soldier's "honour"; Hamlet, the Universe itself; but this making of the stage a battlefield where not the mere politics of the hour, nor yet the vague philosophy of eternity, but the fundamental ethics of society are brought to issue, is surely a quite modern thing. Here indeed the practice of Euripides is an anticipation, not a traceable influence; but the parallel is too vital to be missed.

With such aims it was inevitable that he should be in his methods an unsparing realist,—the first in literature. The legendary Agamemnon "king of men" becomes with him a fickle, well-meaning Sir Politick Would-be; Zeus-born Helen a shallow, vain coquette; the hero of the *Odyssey* a cynical Machiavel. The majesty of tragic buskin and mask

EURIPIDES AND HIS INFLUENCE

he was compelled by stage conventions to retain; but the legends themselves often gave him opportunities of bringing on his heroes with their romantic glamour hidden under a disguise of beggar's rags; and his fondness for this device occasioned that classic passage in Aristophanes [10] where Dicaeopolis, needing a disguise, comes to borrow from Euripides' theatrical stock-in-trade of old clothes. But not only does he bring down the mighty from their seats; he exalts the lowly, the loyal slaves of play after play, the honest yeoman of the *Electra* who shows himself so much more genuinely noble than the neurotic, wolfish children of Agamemnon. With an anticipation of the motto, "Every Man in his Humour down to the Fourth Citizen," he gives even his minor characters character; it is sufficient to contrast for instance the secondary persons of French Classical Tragedy, compared by Coventry Patmore to the brazen automata who waited in the house of Hephaestus. And here too, this "touching of things common," this portrayal, criticized by Sophocles, of men and women, hero and slave, "as they *are*," [11] was to make Euripides the master of later Greek and thence of Roman Comedy. Again,

[18]

comic relief, found occasionally in the tragedies of Æschylus and Sophocles, plays a much larger part with him; and the *Orestes* with its ludicrous Phrygian slave and its happy ending of marriage and reconcilement, the *Alcestis* with its rollicking Heracles, the ironic humour of the *Electra*, the whole light-hearted atmosphere of the *Helen*, which reads like a self-parody, are explorations of a new territory which the dramatists of another age were to make their own. The *Alcestis* looks forward to the *Winter's Tale* and the romantic drama of the Elizabethans.

Next may be considered his general handling of character. First, some stock-parts may be traced back to him: such as the nurse-confidante of the *Medea* and *Hippolytus* (who may be distantly related by way of Seneca to the greatest of all her kind, the nurse of Juliet, not to mention the endless confidantes of the French stage), the ghost, the virgin-martyr, even the villain and the madman. Ghosts indeed of Darius and Clytemnestra appear in Æschylus; but it is rather the prologizing ghost of Polydorus in the *Hecuba* who is the progenitor, again through Seneca with his spectres of Tantalus and Thyestes, of the phantom-armies of the Elizabethans, from the majestic shade of Hamlet to the swarming apparitions of minor Revenge Tragedy such as Chapman's *Revenge of Bussy d'Ambois,* where no less than five ghosts appear at once.

Of the virgin-martyr again there is no nobler example than the Antigone of Sophocles; but in study after study—Macaria, Polyxena, Iphigenia, as well as the older Alcestis and Andromache—Euripides made the theme of woman's self-devotion peculiarly his own; and Renaissance humanism was quick to find in the parallel of Jephthah's daughter with Iphigenia an opportunity of combining the inspiration of Holy Writ and pagan tragedy.

Then too, the melodramatic villain who is so often the real hero of sixteenth-seventeenth century drama is descended both from Machiavelli and from Seneca, the pupil of Euripides. Villains may be divided into two kinds,—"robustious, periwig-pated" villains and cold, calculating villains, Tamburlaines and Iagos. In the one may be recognized the Senecan tyrant, in the other the popular notion of Machiavelli, but not without indebtedness also to the Senecan Odysseus. But Seneca's types are in their turn imitations, or the one hand of the Lycus and Eteocles, on the other of the Odysseus and Menelaus, of the Greek. Still here conjecture must pause; the medieval Mystery, in all innocence of the Classics, had produced in a rudimentary form both rampaging villains like Tiberius and Herod, who "rage" with the fullest stage directions, and sly villains like Judas; and the Elizabethans would have been quite capable of inventing for themselves such obvious types as we have discussed. It is the greatness of their demonstrable indebtedness that makes it so hard to fix where exactly their borrowing stopped.

In the same way and with the same proviso the succession of madmen from Hieronimo in the *Spanish Tragedy* to "Tilburina stark mad in white satin and her confidant stark mad in white linen" in Sheridan's *Critic*, may be followed back to the *Heracles Mad* of Euripides, by way of Seneca's adaptation. Madder indeed than the hero of the latter nothing could be, although the prevailing insanity of almost all that dramatist's characters deprives him of his proper prominence. But in the hypnotism of Pentheus in *The Bacchants* of Euripides, the hallucinations of the hero of the

Orestes and the *Iphigenia in Tauris,* that tireless observer of the minds of men has produced studies of a subtlety unsurpassed for two thousand years to come.[12]

Yet the stage-types of his devising really matter less than the advance he made in the art of individual characterization itself. The persons of Æschylus are Titanic, those of Sophocles heroically ideal; but a subtler psychology, the staging of the struggle, not between man and destiny in the world, but between passion and passion in the soul, begins with Euripides. Æschylus, the forger of iron colossi, the creator of Clytemnestra with her adamantine purpose and yet, with it, that superbly true nervous reaction after the deed is done, knew indeed the human heart. Yet his men and women do not introspect, they act; we do not hear the debate of the two voices in their souls. He was a master of silence as well as of speech; the unspeaking majesty of Prometheus or Niobe, whose grief, like Job's, sits silent through whole scenes, is as noble as the silence of Homer's Ajax to Odysseus in the world below. But the utterance of their conflicting passions by the figures of Euripides, which lets us watch the death-

THE MAN AND HIS WORK

struggle of love and hate in Medea, of passion and shame in Phaedra, is a new and more sophisticated thing. Take for example the scene where Medea is nerving herself to slay her children: [13]

"Ah me! why do you gaze upon me so,
Smiling on me the last of all your smiles,
My little ones? O God! What shall I do?

Women, my heart has failed me, now that I
Have looked on these bright faces of my sons.
I could not do it. Farewell my old resolve,
I'll take my children with me hence from
  Corinth.
What profits it to wring their father's heart
By harming them, and suffer worse myself?
O never, never! So, my plan, farewell.

And yet what ails me? Shall they mock me
  then,
Letting my enemies escape unscathed?
I must endure. O craven heart of mine,
To let such thoughts of weakness steal upon
  thee!
Children, go in—and those that purity
Forbids to share my sacrifice,—why go,
Look to yourselves; I will not stay my hand.

Oh! Oh!
O *heart, my heart, do not, do not this deed,*
Let them go, thou wretch, take pity on thy sons,
In some far land their life shall be thy joy.

No, by the avenging fiends that people Hell,
It shall not be, I will not leave my children
For insolence and outrage to my foes.
Fate wills it so and they cannot escape."

"With Euripides comes in the problem of the divided soul." The mind of Seneca was too vulgar, his psychology too limited to ingenious sophistries and passions pigeon-holed, for him to transmit his master's influence here; Shakespeare and the Elizabethans had to do this work again for themselves; but the lesson of the Greek was not lost upon Racine. Above all in the characters of women,—not indeed the "womanly woman," "fickle and coy" or "ministering angel," of conventional drama,— scarcely two or three have surpassed Euripides.

Of his style little need be said, although its importance in making his influence paramount in antiquity must never be forgotten; for it was partly the simple, flowing ease of his language, his skilful use, according to Wordsworth's precept, of the diction of common life, his lucidity, that enabled him to supersede his two great rivals in the admiration of the ancient world. It is only in occasional narrative passages that his style tends to become, not always successfully, more Æschylean. Another of its qualities, much more distasteful to the modern, but a great additional source of popularity then, is a fondness for the formal cleverness of rhetoric. An audience of Athenians, whose time was lavishly spent either in listening to speeches in court, as jurymen, or in delivering them (for litigants had to conduct their own cases), took a connoisseur's pleasure in wranglings between characters, whether in set tirades or in line-for-line repartee. As usual Seneca exaggerated all he adopted and by the very tawdriness of his epigrams and bombast of his rhetoric captured the ears of the Renaissance with its love of conceits and of "high, astounding terms." But this is only the festering of the lily; and for a fair example of that dignified simplicity praised by Aristotle and by the author of the *Treatise On the Sublime*, take Polyxena's farewell to her mother as she is led away to be sacrificed:

"But *now, O mother dear, give me that hand
I love so well, and lay thy cheek on mine,
Since now for the last time, and then no more,
I see the shining circle of the sun.
Hear me—I ne'er shall speak thy name again,
Mother, O mother, to my death I go.*" [14]

Perhaps the nearest counterpart in English is the style of Shelley in *The Cenci;* its famous and not dissimilar closing words may point the comparison:

"*Give yourself no unnecessary pain,
My dear Lord Cardinal. Here, mother, tie
My girdle for me and bind up this hair
In any simple knot; ay, that does well.
And yours, I see, is coming down. How often
Have we done this for one another. Now
We shall not do it any more. My lord,
We are quite ready.*"

Thus not only did his oratorical qualities make Euripides even in the days of the Empire *the* classic poet of the schools of rhetoric, but this simple directness commended him at once to the fourth century B.C., an age, like the eighteenth A.D., of prose. Even its fanatic Ariphrades,[15] who ridiculed all poetic departures from everyday language, must have disapproved of Euripides far less than of his two great rivals; and not only did later tragedy model its diction on him, but also the New Comedy of Menander, whose fragments are often indistinguishable from his master's; even in an alien tongue this tradition of simple purity was perpetuated by Terence in his turn. Yet, though thus inviting imitation, the simplicity of Euripides proved none too easy to imitate; witness the noble criticism in the *Palatine Anthology:* [16]

*"Seek not to tread where trod Euripides,
Poet; his path is hard for man to take.
Easy it seems: but he that tries its ease,
Shall find it rough with many a thorn and stake.
Scratch not Medea's finger, or thy name
Shall die unwept, unsung. Touch not his fame."*

Such briefly are the main changes made by Euripides in the drama of his time, in its lyric element, in its plot construction, in its characterization and its style. He was trammelled always by the religiously conservative conventions of Attic tragedy; undoubtedly his efforts to create the new helped to destroy the old; and it has been held that he created nothing as precious as what he destroyed.

EURIPIDES AND HIS INFLUENCE

Still some time in that new, more cosmopolitan, more sceptical, more prosaic age, of which he was the herald, the old conventions would have withered just the same; and though some of his changes were unhappy, his practice has been followed, in detail after detail, by the modern world. In his romantic love-interest, his freer intermingling of comedy with tragedy, he looks forward to Shakespeare; in his subtle penetration of the passionate human heart to Racine; in his fervour for intellectual honesty, his worship of Truth even above Beauty, to Ibsen and the only living drama of the nineteenth century.

After Euripides the dramatist there remains Euripides the thinker,—the subject to-day of a vast and growing literature, much of it vitiated by disregard of an obvious principle, which book after book recognizes in theory in its first chapter, and ignores in all that follows. You cannot credit a dramatist indiscriminately with the opinions of his characters; this mistake is as old as the poet's own audiences, who seem to have been in some ways quite peculiarly imbecile, so that "immoral utterances" like Hippolytus' (612) "With my tongue I swore it—never with my heart," [17] or praise of money in another play, were greeted with bellows of righteous indignation. A second principle, hardly even recognized in dealing with Euripides, is that one cannot pin down any poet to a cast-iron and unalterable conviction about the views he expresses even when speaking in his own person, on the ultimate questions of life. As Walt Whitman says:

> "*Do I contradict myself?*
> *Very well then I contradict myself.*
> *I am large, I contain multitudes.*"

Thus of Swinburne, to take a single instance, it would be possible to argue by quotations from his works that he believed in personal survival after death, in a vaguer kind of dreamy immortality, or in complete annihilation. Similarly Euripides on God or the Soul, on Fate or Freewill, on the justice of the Universe,—even when he seems most personal, is often self-contradictory. He might have cried with *Piers Plowman*:

"*The more I muse thereinne, the mistier it seemeth,*

And the depper I devyne, the derker me it thynketh."

He shared the sceptical wisdom of Socrates, the knowledge of his ignorance—*se moquer de la philosophie, c'est vraiment philosopher;* his agnosticism works mainly as an engine of destruction, and *"écrasez l'infâme"* was as much his war cry as Voltaire's.[18] The orthodox religion disgusted him; it is fantastic to believe with Verrall, that its destruction was the main object with which he wrote his tragedies; but the inexorable fact, veiled so long by the glamour of beautiful legend,—that if the gods behaved as the stories said, they were fiend and fool in one,—he drags to light, in play after play. Sometimes he is contented with a *reductio ad absurdum* of deities, like the Apollo of the *Electra* who drives children to matricide for the sake of a fatuous revenge, or him of the *Ion* who first violates a girl and then deserts her; or the Aphrodite of the *Hippolytus* blasting in childish pique three human lives; or the sinister powers of the *Trojan Women* indifferently ordaining the misery of mortals nobler than themselves. Sometimes he symbolizes under the shape of traditional gods the wild forces of the world, "the gods behind the gods"—the eternal virginity of Nature in the Artemis of the *Hippolytus*, the pitiless onrush of the forces of life in the Dionysus of *The Bacchants*. It signifies nothing that some of his characters give edifying expression to all the orthodox beliefs; it was not such blunted relics of the past that would remain fixed in the memory of his audience as they filed out of the theatre beneath Athena's hill, but barbed utterances by the quiverful, such as the retort of his Auge, mother of a child by Heracles, to Athena's self,—words quoted in after years by Clement of Alexandria against the old religion:

*"The spoils of slaughtered men
Make glad thine eyes, red wreckage of the slain,—
Thou call'st not them unclean. But this my babe
Thou deemest horrible,"*

or such as the protest of Heracles himself in the play called by his name:

*"I cannot think gods love adultery;
Nay, ever have I scorned and ever will
To hold that they cast chains on one another,*

*Or one of them is born another's lord.
For God, if God indeed, can lack for naught,—
These things are only bards' unhappy tales"* [19]

"He has made men think that there are no gods" is the complaint of Aristophanes; and "atheist" is the curt epithet that echoes through antiquity, countenanced by utterances like Bellerophon's famous:

"*Does any say that there are gods in Heaven?
None, none, none!*" [20]

Yet of his own view all one can surmise is that it was a belief in "a sort of something," subject to the variations of a poet's moods, a vague theism, though he makes his Moving Cause now Mind, now the Ether, now Necessity. In any justice in the world's governance he trusts even less; the classic passage in the *Trojan Women* is often quoted as if it were his last word:

"*O base of earth and on the earth enthroned,
Whoe'er Thou art, so hard for thought to find,
O Zeus, or Nature's Law, or Mind of Man,
I praise Thee, since by silent ways Thou bringest
All mortal things to justice in the end.*" [21]

But the speech must not be taken without its context, the splendour without the irony; for this lyric justice proves at a touch but mockery; and the guilty Helen passes from the stage to be happy ever after, while the children of Troy, her victims, are dragged from their smoking ruins to slavery or the sword. *"Il y a horriblement de mal sur la terre,"* and the poet's view of life is darkened by that profound pessimism, which even those who do not share it must admit to have produced more of the world's great literature, from *Ecclesiastes* to Thomas Hardy, than all the *Te Deums* of the optimist.

And after life? Here too "we drift on legends ever," and though he speaks sometimes of recompense to come, he speaks also and perhaps more certainly of eternal sleep; and it is for this, rather than the horrors of immortality, that his Macaria prays before her sacrifice.[22] As for second-sight and prophecy, he calls them fraud with no hesitating voice.[23]

> *"This is but folly*
> *To think the flight of birds can profit men. . . .*
> *'Tis a mere plot to cozen all our lives;*
> *Judgment and Wisdom are the truest seers."* [24]

He hesitates, again, between Free Will and Determinism; and in Ethics his scepticism brings him at moments to echo the relativity of Protagoras. Man is his own measure—"What deed is base, if the doer deems not so?" Only to the splendour of courage and the grace of pity is he never cold.

> "Ah Pity does not dwell with Ignorance,
> But with the wise of men; so Wisdom's self
> Must suffer pain for being overgreat." [25]

"His plays," says Lecky, "had been to the ancient world the first revelation of the supreme beauty of the gentler virtues"; and "la pitié"—adds Anatole France, "la pitié, M. le Professeur, c'est le fond même du génie." Sixteen centuries after, St. Thomas Aquinas was including the spectacle of the tortures of the damned among the joys of the Christian Heaven.

On political and social questions Euripides shows the same fearless freedom of thought; and if here too he seems to take now one position, now another, it is not only because he is a dramatist, but because he recognizes that truth is greater than consistency and that "the Golden Rule is that there is no Golden Rule." In politics, like Thucydides, he hated alike the rule of the many and of the few, and his sympathies were with the unspoilt yeoman middle-class. But strongly individualist above all, he protests incessantly against the politician's parrot-cry of the "common good," the invocation of the Moloch of the State to wreck the single life. To initiate a war of senseless conquest the girl Iphigenia is murdered at Aulis; to secure its sterile fruits the boy Astyanax is flung from the shattered towers of Troy. But it is in his attitude to war that he is most advanced; he upheld indeed in *The Heracleidae* and *The Suppliants* an Athens doing battle for the weak; but the conventional glories of war he never spared, and Plutarch relates that his praises of Peace in the *Erechtheus* helped to bring the Athenian people to make the peace of Nicias. It was this freedom from national prejudice, shared by him with Socrates, "the citizen of the world," that made him the sympathetic delineator of barbarian and slave, that was to make him hereafter the favourite of the cosmopolitan world of the Roman Empire,—the poet of the Gentiles.

"*Unto the eagle all the Heaven is free,
To the noble heart the whole wide earth is home.*" [26]

Of his misogyny sufficient nonsense has already been written. That such a charge could be seriously brought against the creator of Alcestis and Phaedra, Macaria and Polyxena, Andromache and Creusa and Iphigenia, is merely ludicrous; it was possible, not so much because he also depicted women with bad characters as because he dwelt on women's characters at all. He made them subtle and gave them brains and therewith the knowledge of evil as well as good; and if this seems to resemble the Serpent's dealings with Eve,—well, there is a great deal to be said for the Serpent. We find indeed no proof [27] in Euripides of Plato's desire to bring women from the Oriental seclusion [28] of the Athenian home, to work on equal terms with men; but he does urge that there should be one moral law for both sexes; and he was certainly a pioneer in regarding women, not as children, not as odalisques, but as adults for good or ill. The true misogyny is indifference. "There is nothing more precious," says one of his characters, "than a woman who is a comrade"—συμπαθής; and if much evil, too, is spoken of them in the plays, it is because under the social conventions of the time women were bred to be frivolous and deceitful and vain. If things were so, it was not Euripides who would pretend they were comfortably otherwise; and he had the saving grace of humour enough to parody his own invective in the *Cyclops* (186-7).

Such was Euripides the thinker. The laurel-wreath, of which Heine speaks in the sentence that heads this chapter, none will deny him; but he too, like Heine, came with a sword, not with the immortal peace of Sophocles, upon the stage of Athens,—though only, as it may have seemed to his contemporaries, in the end to lose the day. Yet the morrow, the centuries to come, were his. It is no "old, unhappy, far-off thing," this struggle in which he died. It rages to-day; it will to the world's end, while men have minds to change and courage to change them. Mankind has, Janus-like, two faces. Some look back, for the world seems to darken before them:

"*But to me your new device is barren, the days are bare,*

> *Things long past over suffice, and men forgotten that were."*

So felt Aristophanes and the larger half of Athens, seeing in Euripides, as in Socrates, a revolutionary and a corrupter. But it is to others that to-morrow belongs; they know that to stay still is to drift backwards, that "one good custom," grown old and rotten, will "corrupt the world." It is an easy faith for youth; few old men have kept it; but Euripides was one.

> *"Wouldst thou that I should tell soft lies to thee, Or rugged truth? Speak,—'tis for thee to choose;"* [29]

so one of the fragments runs. In his own steadfast answer, his loyalty always to light and freedom, lies his claim to honour not only among the great dramatists, but also among the great men of the world. Courage was his, and pity.

II. THE INFLUENCE OF EURIPIDES ON ANTIQUITY

> "If I am not too partial to myself, a variety of anecdote can be displeasing to no one, unless he is peevish enough to rival the superciliousness of Cato."
> WILLIAM OF MALMESBURY

IN his own age and country Euripides had suffered the prophet's fate. He gained no doubt a minority of strong partisans; the absurd Dionysus of the *Frogs* takes his plays to read at sea, like Froude in after days, and owns to being "more than silly" about him; but all his life Athens grudged him recognition or success, and it says much in itself that the old man of seventy-two should set forth to lay his bones in foreign earth, whether or no, as one story says, "because of the malicious glee of almost everyone" at some misfortune that befell him. The greatest city in Hellas could be strangely parochial at times.

Of his famous fellow-Athenians a few seem to have shown some appreciation, Sophocles, Socrates, and perhaps Thucydides. Sophocles' criticism of his rival's realism, quoted above, and his broad pleasantries about discrepancies in Euripides' theory and practice of misogyny, even if they are not inventions, signify little compared with his genuine tributes; he imitated the Euripidean prologue in his *Women of Trachis* and the *deus ex machina* in his *Philoctetes;* and, on the news of the death in Macedon, the chorus of Sophocles appeared dressed in mourning at the preliminary tragic show.

Socrates again is persistently linked with Euripides by a tradition, which cannot be entirely discounted except by that type of scholar who refuses to believe any facts about antiquity which he has not himself invented. Socrates is said to have attended no tragedies except his friend's; [30] he is even related (on the more than dubious authority of comic poets) to have collaborated in them. So strong a tradition can hardly be quite unfounded; both men were agnostics and seekers, never weary of discussing the nature of God and good; and though Euripides knew the nature of man too well to have accepted the facile Socratic "Virtue is Knowledge" with its blindness to the reasonless depths of human passion, yet both

THE INFLUENCE OF EURIPIDES

were true heralds of the coming age of cosmopolitanism and philosophy.

But one contemporary voice drowns all the rest with its ceaseless torrent of anger and disgust and scorn—Aristophanes. The yelpings of other comic poets time has stilled; but in his plays we have the record of a truceless war of twenty years on the irreligion, the "highbrow" immorality, the ragged realism, the ridiculous lyrics, the musical affectations, the dialogue, —now bombast, now chatter—the doggerel prologues, of Euripides. He studied the hated master with the assiduity of a Boswell; he admired, even to the point of imitation, his style; but not even in death did he give his victim rest. The *Frogs* in the very next year (405) contains the fullest and wittiest attack of all; and its verdict is—"His works have perished with him." [31]

Never in the history of criticism was a falser forecast. Only two months later Aristophanes was to see the trilogy containing the *Iphigenia in Aulis* and *The Bacchants* posthumously victorious at the Great Dionysia. Already the reaction had begun; and though Archelaus refused to give back the poet's body, Athens raised him a cenotaph inscribed, it is said, with an epitaph, the work of Thucydides or of Timotheus the musician:

> "Euripides all Hellas for his monument hath won,
>   Though he lies where last he rested, in fields of Macedon.
>   Yet the heart of Hellas bore him, e'en Athens; and he thrilled
>   The world with such sweet singing, with his praise the world is filled."

Abroad, however, men did not wait to praise Euripides till his ears were stopped with dust. The king of Macedon showed his guest a deferential admiration that even familiarity does not seem to have blunted. Apollo at Delphi, says tradition, replied in an iambic distich to Chaerephon, the friend of Socrates:

> "Sophocles is wise, wiser Euripides,
>   But Socrates is wisest of them all." [32]

Above all the rival of Athens in the west, Syracuse, whither Euripides is said to have once gone on embassy, idolized the work of this alien enemy. In *Balaustion's Adventure* Browning has made familiar the tale of the Caunian ship that, pirate-chased, was refused

THE INFLUENCE OF EURIPIDES

refuge in the port of Syracuse, as belonging to an Athenian dependency, until quick questioning revealed that some on board knew verses of Euripides. Equally well-known is the story [33] that at the close of the disastrous siege survivors of the Athenian army were for the same cause given life, even liberty, by the victors, and

"*Returning home to Athens, sought him out,*
The old bard in the solitary house,
And thanked him ere they went to sacrifice."

A few years later free Syracuse lay beneath the heel of Dionysius, but the tyrant here at least did not reverse the judgment of his countrymen and, author of bad tragedies himself, bought for a great price the tablets, pen, and lyre of the dead master, to dedicate them at the shrine of the Muses in his capital.

Meanwhile the influence of the dead poet already begins to play a living part in the last struggles of Athens herself. Thus a strange tale [34] hangs round her last desperate victory of Arginusae in the year he died. Thrasyllus the Athenian commander dreamt that he and six of his colleagues were in the theatre at home, acting in the *Phœnician Women* of Euripides, while the enemy generals competed against them in his *Suppliants*,—both tragedies dealing with the legend of The Seven against Thebes. He and his fellows were victorious, but perished themselves like the seven champions. The dream, which the story makes oddly plausible by its very confusedness, of course came true, the successful generals being put to death by a grateful country on the charge of negligence in rescuing their shipwrecked crews. Two years later (404) the city fell and, Plutarch [35] tells, the proposal that her people should be sold as slaves and Athens made an abomination of desolation, a grazing-ground for sheep, was only defeated by a sudden storm of pity that swept the gathered leaders, as they heard a man of Phocis singing the opening chorus of the *Electra*:

"O *Agamemnon's child,*
  I *am come, Electra, to thy homestead in the wild.*"

Here of course, as at Syracuse, it was doubtless as much the air as the words, that so mastered the hearts of men. But how sentimental

[44]

these old Greeks were! When our statesmen meet to deal peace to the vanquished, whatever may ail their judgment, none can say their hearts ever suffered from such generous weakness as this.

From this point down to the beginning of the Middle Ages Euripides remains the supreme tragic poet, almost the supreme poet, of the whole Greek world. There are said to be more quotations in later literature from his *Orestes* than from all the extant works of Æschylus and Sophocles; and more quotations from Euripides as a whole than from any other poets except Homer and Menander. Thus the famous lines of the lost *Cresphontes,*

*"In truth we ought to gather and bewail
The babe new-born into this world of pain,
But him that's dead and rested from his toils
Speed with all joy and blessing on his way,"* [36]

are cited "by Cicero, Strabo, Seneca, Dio Chrysostom, Plutarch, Sextus Empiricus, Clement of Alexandria, Theodoretus, Aristides, Menander (the rhetorician), and Procopius." Phrases of his became proverbial, for instance —the "Sparta is yours, make the most of Sparta," of the *Telephus,* which in its Latin dress is still familiar although it has lost its old implication—"mind your own business"; and in general his tendency after his death in some degree to supersede even Homer in the Greek world has been compared by Eduard Meyer with Goethe's displacement of the Bible in nineteenth-century Germany. His real effect indeed on the later centuries of Hellenism is not to be appraised in terms of the quotations and imitations that crowd these pages. He influenced not only Menander or Plutarch but Menander's audience and Plutarch's public in ways we cannot know; his view of life is partly the cause, still more the forerunner of the spirit of the Hellenistic world, so enlightened, so common sense, so kindly and urbane in its gentlemanly attitude towards social inferiors as well as equals. It is the humanity that breathes alike in the new-found plays of Menander and in Lucian's description of Demonax. It rests on no buoyant, young vitality, it shows no wild heroism; we shall find no more the moral passion of Euripides; for the battle is won and an age of gentle scepticism smiles at the gods he fought against and welcomes the enlightened humanity for which he pleaded. And the later philosophers, Stoic and Sceptic, concerned far less with the nature of the universe than with the duty of man, greet in him the subtle psychologist, the tireless reasoner on the ethics of common sense. We cannot measure how much he moulded the popular ideas of those generations; we can only note how he lives on the lips of their spokesmen, of the philosophers down to Marcus Aurelius and Plotinus and of the heralds of the new religion, for whom he had so well paved the way, from St. Paul to Clement of Alexandria.

The fourth century is the great age of Greek philosophy, of the Orators, of the New Comedy; on all three Euripides has left his mark. In a famous chorus of the *Medea* there is indeed what has been fancifully, but not altogether unreasonably, called a prophecy of the Platonic Academy with its union of Love and Wisdom; it describes how Cypris, Our Lady of the gardens by fair-flowing Cephisus, where the "Academy" was to be founded,

"Sends forth her Loves to share in Wisdom's throne
And help make all life nobler."

But whether Plato here recognized himself or no, the philosopher had, as he grew older, no use for poets except as vile bodies for the moralist's dissection; and though he quotes Euripides and speaks of him as "preëminent in tragedy," it is with no cordiality. He may have deigned to take from the *Alcestis* (254) the call of fate to the doomed Socrates in the *Phaedo* (115A), from the lost *Philoctetes* (*Fr.* 787) the choice by Odysseus of a happy obscurity before all other lives in the Vision of Er which closes *The Republic* (620C), from the *Hippolytus* (525-64) the comparison of Love to a buzzing, stinging creature of the air (*Republic* 573A) [37]; he may have cited him like scripture, as in the story [38] which tells how Plato refused Dionysius' offer of a purple robe with a line of *The Bacchants* (836) condemning effeminacy, whereupon Aristippus the Hedonist, with his usual good sense, accepted the finery, capping the quotation with another (316-7) from the same play to the effect that true worth was not so easily corrupted. But the philosopher had only a hysterical hatred for the emotions which fascinated the playwright and their views of life could never meet. The fantastic belief in "Virtue as Knowledge" could never accept a Phaedra or a Medea "knowing the better, choosing the worse"; [39] and in *The Republic* (568A), with a distortion as silly as dishonest, Plato brings forward, as a ground for excluding Euripides and his like from the ideal state, the charge of "extolling tyrants." These less pleasant sides of the most charming of philosophers are usually passed over; but there is no reason why the Puritan spirit towards art should be recognized for the unclean thing it is, when it smashes stained glass or scolds in the thick accents of a Stephen Gosson, but not when it speaks with the silver tongue of Plato. He need not have been so exercised about excluding the poets from his Republic; few would ever have craved admission to that dismal barrack; fortunately for his work's survival there was one poet of whom Plato all his life could never quite get rid,—himself.

Aristotle as usual is saner and less eloquent. He both quotes and criticizes. A citation from the *Melanippe* (*Fr.* 486) crowns the famous praise of Justice in the *Ethics* (1129 B, 15): "Therefore it seems that Justice is the chief of all virtues and more wonderful 'than is the star of evening or of dawn.'" Again he is said to have justified his appearance as a rival rhetorician to Isocrates with a parody of the

Euripidean verse: "Shame to sit dumb and let barbarians talk," in which the name of Isocrates was substituted in the uncomplimentary place. In definite criticism he wrote a work, now lost, on *Problems in Euripides;* elsewhere (*Rhet.*, 3. 2.) he praises his happy invention of a style made natural by borrowing from the diction of everyday; and in the *Poetics*, while criticizing him for irrelevancy of chorus, weakness of structure, occasional exaggeration or inconsistency of characterization, he awards him that title of fame—"most tragic of the poets."

The orators reflect the poet less. He is quoted by Demosthenes,[40] by Æschines[41] who calls him "a poet as wise as any," and by Lycurgus[42] who cites a long speech from the *Erechtheus*, as persevering moderns rehearse Gaunt's dying utterance from *Richard II*, for its model patriotism. Lycurgus, however, is more important as author of a law (c. 330 B.C.) ordering an official text of the plays of Æschylus, Sophocles, and Euripides to be prepared and faithfully followed in those revivals of their works which had become a regular institution. For as in the eighteenth century with Garrick's productions of Shakespeare, acting

THE INFLUENCE OF EURIPIDES

advanced while play-writing decayed and the actors of tragedy in the fourth century are almost more famous than its authors. The supremacy of Euripides by this time is witnessed by an inscription [43] referring to the revival of old tragedies, one annually, from 341 to 339 B.C., the year before the loss of Athenian liberty on the field of Chaeroneia; all three recorded are his.

Of course new tragedies as well continued to be produced throughout the fourth century, —"heads without name no more remembered." Euripides was their great model; his style, his rhetoric, his subtleties the new generation might learn, but not his secret. It was not on the tragedy of the century, but on its comedy, above all on Menander, that the mantle of Euripides had really fallen. The indebtedness to him of the New Comedy with its Romantic motifs and yet urbane realism of speech, its wronged virgins and long-lost heirs, and its understanding of the human heart was already recognized by ancient critics; indeed it was recognized by the poets themselves. They quote him by name; to Nicostratus he is "dearest Euripides," "who in one line has summed all human life"; Diphilus calls him

"Euripides the golden," Philemon, "Euripides the one man eloquent"; and the last-named in a well-known fragment makes one of his characters exclaim:

"Ah, if the dead indeed had consciousness,
I had hanged myself to see Euripides."

As for Menander, the greatest of them all, his indebtedness is emphasized by Quintilian (X. 1. 69.) and his fragments are often indistinguishable. Small wonder that this rage should have excited two comedies, both called *The Euripides-worshipper*, satirizing, like Gilbert and Sullivan's *Patience*, the fashionable cult of the day. It was a cosmopolitan age; the old patriotisms had perished; and when one of its young men was asked "Of what city are you?" it was thought witty of him to reply "I have a comfortable income." Terence's "I am a man—nothing in mankind is foreign to me" is an expression of the same attitude in a nobler mood. For such a world Æschylus was too Titanic, Sophocles too Attic; with the universality of Homer Euripides alone could compare.

And so in the active life, not less than in the literature, of the time he holds his place.

THE INFLUENCE OF EURIPIDES

Alexander, the ruthless lord of Pherae (died 359 B.C.), leaves the theatre, like Hamlet's uncle, in the middle of a performance of *The Trojan Women,* and, with a considerateness strange for him to show, sends word to the actor that he had no fault to find with the acting, but was ashamed that men should see weeping for Hecuba one who had watched dry-eyed the agony of so many victims of his own.[44] Isocrates "the old man eloquent," his gray hairs brought in sorrow to the grave by "that dishonest victory" of Macedon at Chaeroneia (338 B.C.), dies quoting the first lines of three plays of Euripides which tell of three ancient enslavements of Hellas.[45] Timoleon, the Corinthian deliverer of Sicily, puts to death his captured enemy Euthymus for having cited in a scornful speech Medea's words about "Corinthian *women* coming out of doors."[46] But it is in the life of Alexander of Macedon himself, founder of a new world and very emblem of triumphant Hellenism rolling back its boundaries to the Jaxartes and the Indus, that the living influence of Euripides at this time can best be traced. Through the tragedy of that brief and brilliant life phrases of the dead Athenian run like a *leit-motiv*. His mother Olympias had herself been a very Agave, celebrating the rites of Bacchus with great serpents twined about her; and when, years after, King Philip put her away and wedded Cleopatra, niece of his general Attalus, she showed herself a very Medea. History has been rightly distrustful of the whisper that one of her greatest heroes was a parricide; but the story [47] goes that when the intending assassin came to sound Alexander, the prince only muttered the line (228) in which Medea resolves the death

"Of groom and bride and father of the bride."

At all events it was the dagger of his mother's creature that brought him to the throne. In the conquest of Asia Euripides like Homer was part of Alexander's field-library [48]; and at the fatal revel where the drunken king murdered his friend Clitus with his own hand, the final provocation was given by that friend's recital of the bitter lines of the *Andromache* [49] (693 ff.):

*"Alas how foul a custom 'tis in Hellas
That, when an army comes in triumph home,*

THE INFLUENCE OF EURIPIDES

*Men praise not those that bore the brunt of battle,
But to the general all the glory goes."*

Afterwards when Alexander's own hour was at hand, and the Chaldeans warned him not to set foot in Babylon, he answered in the sceptic-poet's mocking words (*Fr.* 973)

"The best of seers is he that guesses best;" [50]

and at the last of all his feasts he recited a part from the *Andromeda*.[51] He died, his work half-done; but "in Persia, in Susiana, in Gedrosia," says Plutarch, strange Eastern tongues were learning to lisp Euripides.[52]

We pass to the third century, the age of Alexander's successors, of the literary learning and learned literature of Alexandria, of the second wave of Greek philosophy,—Stoic, Sceptic, and Epicurean. Where Plato had cavilled and Aristotle freely criticized, the later philosophers enthusiastically admired. To Crantor [53] Homer and Euripides were the greatest of all poets; in times of sorrow he found solace in repeating the words of Bellerophon:

"Alas! Yet why alas? Man's life is thus."

And he wooed the young Arcesilas to be his pupil with Perseus' words to Andromeda, to which the youth replied with the heroine's happy cry of self-surrender.[54] Crates was moved to take up the asceticism of the Cynic by a performance of the *Telephus;* Zeno the founder of Stoicism had ever on his lips the lines of *The Suppliants* which describe the noble Capaneus; and his successor Chrysippus had incorporated so much of the *Medea* in his own work that one of his readers, when asked what he was studying, answered with absent-minded truthfulness, "The *Medea* of Chrysippus." [55]

The grammarians of Alexandria collected and edited the plays; tragedians of the Alexandrian Pleiad, like the unintelligible Lycophron, imitated them. Another of these latter, Alexander the Ætolian,[56] has left a fragment of verse contrasting the personal gloom of Euripides with "the Siren sweetness and honey" of his poetry. Of the Ptolemies themselves, Philopator borrowed from the *Andromeda* for his tragedy *Adonis;* and Euergetes in the second century obtained from Athens the loan of the official text of the three tragedians, and then chose to forfeit his security of fifteen

THE INFLUENCE OF EURIPIDES

talents rather than return it. In other fields too of Alexandrian literature springs up the seed of Euripides; the Medea of Apollonius Rhodius, to whom Virgil's Dido was to owe much, is not indeed greatly influenced by the tragedy; but this has certainly helped to inspire the wild forsaken witch-maiden of Theocritus' second *Idyll,* while traces of *The Bacchants* and perhaps of the *Cyclops* can be seen in *Idylls XXVI* and *VIII.*

Lastly to this age of Alexander's successors belongs the burlesque tale of Lucian, how the people of Abdera in Thrace, city famous for its obtuseness, being visited one summer by a strolling company who played the *Andromeda,* caught tragedy-fever so badly that the streets were filled with wild, pale figures declaiming: "O Love, high lord both over gods and men!" until the autumn frosts cooled them back to sanity again.[57] The popularity of Euripides in the third century B.C. in Greece is also proved by an inscription which mentions the singing, in the Delphic stadium, of the "Dionysus" chorus and a lyre-solo from *The Bacchants* of Euripides.[58]

At the same time begins the working of Euripides in a greater and less sentimental

EURIPIDES AND HIS INFLUENCE

city than Abdera. For in the year 240 B.C., Rome, mistress now of the Greater Greece of South Italy and Sicily, saw her first adaptation of Greek tragedy.

At this point, however, before we turn westward, a word may be said of the effect of the plays on Greek and Græco-Roman Art. It is interesting to watch Euripides tending to replace Homer as the great source of subjects on fourth century vases, especially in South Italy; and in painting proper we hear of a picture of the death of Polyxena in the Propylaea at Athens, of a "Death of Pentheus" in the temple of Dionysus, of a "Sacrifice of Iphigenia" (which is reflected in the famous Pompeian painting and in a mosaic in Spain), and of a study of Satyrs measuring the length of the Cyclops' hugh thumb, both by Timanthes (about 400 B.C). Of course in cases like these direct indebtedness to the poet is often only a possibility. Again Timomachus (first century B.C.) painted an "Orestes," an "Iphigenia in Tauris," and a "Medea" so lifelike in the agony of her indecision that it was bought for a fabulous sum by Julius Caesar. This last, like many other Euripidean scenes, reappears among the wall-paintings of Pom-

THE INFLUENCE OF EURIPIDES

peii. Lastly Philostratus (third century A.D.) describes pictures, whether real or imaginary, of the mad Heracles and of the death of Hippolytus, with his beloved mountains mourning for him in the shapes of women, and the meadows, in a Pateresque vision, as young men casting down their faded flowers.[59]

In sculpture, Etruscan sarcophagi [60] (fourth-second century B.C.) reproduce scenes often in loving detail, from such plays as the *Hippolytus, Iphigenia, Telephus, Medea, Andromeda;* and similarly, but with a special fondness for the *Hippolytus,* Roman sarcophagi of the first and second centuries A.D. Of more famous works it must suffice to recall the Maenad of Scopas and that sculptured drum from the temple of Artemis at Ephesus now in the British Museum, which is supposed to represent Hermes handing over Alcestis to Death, a beautiful sad youth (both, fourth century B.C.), the Pasitelean "Electra and Orestes" with its slight Euripidean suggestion of her ragged clothing (first century B.C.), and the famous "Farnese Bull" of Apollonius and Tauriscus, a florid stone whirlwind representing the catastrophe of the *Antiope* with some of the crudity of the "Laocoön," although

[59]

softened by romantic attempts, as in the Hippolytus picture described above, to symbolize the natural features of the scene.

On the tragedy of the Roman Republic there is not here space to dwell. It survives only in fragments, although Cicero thought it one of the glories of Rome and Quintilian ranked it above the comedy of Plautus and Terence. But it remained always a derivative and somewhat alien thing, until finally its place was taken by mime and pantomime and gladiator. And yet it has its importance because it helped to familiarize the Roman people with the legends of Greece and to educate the public of Catullus and Virgil. Of the plays of the five chief tragic dramatists of the Republic,—two pioneers, Livius Andronicus and Naevius, and three masters, Ennius, Pacuvius, and Accius,— seven, in Ribbeck's collection, are based on Æschylus, sixteen on Sophocles, and no less than twenty-four on Euripides, whose influence, as the most cosmopolitan and simple of the three, is not only the widest, but the earliest, so that it appears in thirteen out of fifteen tragedies of Ennius. These works were not of course mere translations; the Roman left his stamp on the most Greek of originals; and the

THE INFLUENCE OF EURIPIDES

poetry of Athens becomes shortened to a prosaic curtness or expanded into a roll of Latin thunder, the pathos and lamentation of Hellas hardened to the iron resolution of the legion. Thus the chorus of Ennius' *Iphigenia* is composed not of women but of veterans; the simple directness of Medea's

"*Women of Corinth, I am come abroad*" (214)

becomes in Latin the sonorous

"*Dwellers in Corinth's towering citadel,
Ladies of great possessions, lineage high;*" [61]

while Creon's threat

"*If God's next coming lamp of dawn behold
Thee and thy sons within the bounds of Corinth,
Thou diest*" (352 ff.)

is whittled down to

"*If I find thee here upon the morrow morn,
Thou diest*" (*Fr.* 311).

Another point of interest is the influence of the scepticism of Euripides on Roman tragedy; Ennius, Pacuvius, and Accius all have passages in mockery of soothsaying like the following from Pacuvius (*Fr.* 35):

*"But as for those that know the speech of birds
And learn more from a sheep's heart than their own,
They should be rather heard than listened to."*

In the last decades of the Republic Roman Tragedy dwindles down to mere literary drama meant mainly for reading rather than the stage; but through the turbulence of the age of Cicero, made so vivid still across two thousand years by its wealth of literary remains, reappears the influence of Euripides, not so much indeed in the new literature as in the life of the time. Thus Lucretius in his crowning instance of the curse of the orthodox religion, the description of the sacrifice of Iphigenia at Aulis, uses the play;[62] and elsewhere (II. 991 ff.) he closely renders an Anaxagorean chorus from the *Chrysippus* (*Fr.* 839) on the birth of all things from earth and air, and their dissolution back again. Cicero himself is steeped in Euripides; his philosophic works are full of extracts translated into Latin verse; his letters are dotted with the half-finished

THE INFLUENCE OF EURIPIDES

quotations which mark extreme familiarity, as if he agreed with the judgment of his brother Quintus, "I think his lines so many oracles"; and, last of all, it is told that he was reading the *Medea* in his litter, when (43 B.C.) the assassins of Antony overtook and cut him down. Indeed all this tragic stage of the death of the Republic is haunted by the shade of Euripides. Already Cicero's old enemy, Crassus, colleague of Caesar and Pompey in the First Triumvirate, had played his life's last part in another Euripidean play. Trapped with his legions by the Parthian horsemen in the sands of Syria (53 B.C.) he was captured and slain. It happened that before the Kings Artavasdes of Armenia and Orodes of Parthia Greek strolling players were acting *The Bacchants;* as the play reached its close, where Agave bears the severed head of Pentheus in triumph home, the head of Crassus arrived from the army at the front; and the actor, Jason of Tralles, changing his stage-property for the blood-stained reality, chanted afresh Agave's triumph-song,—Greek degradation lending itself to the shame of Rome before the savage East.[63]

So Caesar,[64] too, all his life kept on his

tongue the lines of Eteocles in *The Phoenician Women,* marked by Cicero [65] with special disapproval:

*"If wrong must be, 'twere best a man should do it
To win a crown, and in all else be just"* (524–5);

and Brutus, before his death, in the bitterness of defeat at Philippi cried, says tradition, for the vengeance of Heaven, in the same poet's [66] words:

"God, be not blind to him that caused these things" (*Medea,* 332),

while his last utterance of all was, says Cassius Dio (XLVII. 49. 2), that fragment of despair, by an author unknown, but surely Euripides:

*"Unhappy virtue, thou wast but a name,
It seems, though I in very deed pursued thee,—
And thou but Fortune's thrall!"*

Whence Lord Chesterfield's cruel remark on Henry Fox, that "he lived, as Brutus died, calling virtue a name."

So passed the Republic; but its heir, the cold

THE INFLUENCE OF EURIPIDES

Augustus,[67] like its destroyer, Caesar, could not apparently get through life without his Euripidean motto. Taken from the same play, almost the same page, as the dictator's, it presents a ludicrous, yet characteristic, contrast:

"Better far the prudent soldier than the bold."
  (*Phoenissae,* 599.)

As different in its turn is the amiable

"Once I am dead, let earth be wrapt in flame"
  (*author unknown*)

or "After me the deluge," attributed to Tiberius, who proved also sufficiently sensitive to Euripides to put to death Mamercus Scaurus for embodying in a play of his own yet another line of *The Phoenician Women* (393)

"We must bear the folly of the powers that be,"—

which he took as a personal insult.[68] From all this anecdotage it should at least be clear that Euripides still meant a good deal in various ways to men in the Rome of the late Republic and early Empire.

[65]

EURIPIDES AND HIS INFLUENCE

On the actual literature of the Augustan age his influence is not at first sight very apparent, though far stronger than in the preceding generation. Virgil's indebtedness, most clearly seen in the first six books of the *Aeneid,* is a matter rather of ideas than of phrases, although the familiar "Forsan et haec olim meminisse juvabit" has a forgotten origin or at least anticipation in a fragment of Euripides.[69] From the *Trojan Women* Virgil has taken here and there a pathetic touch in Aeneas' story of the sack of Troy,[70] from the *Orestes* his hero's impulse to slay the guilty Helen.[71] In book III the *Hecuba* provides him with the story of Priam's son Polydorus, murdered for his gold by the Thracian king, and the close of the *Andromache* leaves that heroine where Aeneas finds her, queen of Molossia and wed to Helenus. Again in the later half of the poem we find both an allusion to the *Hippolytus,* when its hero's son takes his place in the gathering of the Italian clans,[72] and an echo of it in Diana's lament for the death of Camilla,[73]— herself just such another virgin soul whom Our Lady of Wild Things loved but could not save. Yet these touches are trifling compared with the debt of Dido to Euripides.

Her tragedy has always been one of the problems of Virgilian criticism. Why does the poet make his hero a false and heartless betrayer? "Aeneas had a Roman sense of duty"—"Dido was a Carthaginian, an enemy-queen." Such explanations explain nothing. Why are we compelled to feel both that Aeneas did not really care about Dido and that Virgil did—intensely?

I can only believe one explanation. Dido seduced from his first faith to Rome not only the hero, but the poet himself; in her, Virgil conjured up a spirit fairer than he had the heart to bind. The hand of a dead master guided his pen and the ghosts of a vanished stage rose to sit on that throne in Carthage; in Dido are reincarnate the Phaedra and the Medea of Euripides. In her struggle with her rising passion she is no doubt nearest to the Medea of Apollonius Rhodius; but at the end when her love turns to hate, we recognize the fire and the pity of the tragedian. As for Virgil's hero, the shape is the shape of the 'pious' Aeneas, but the voice becomes Jason's. Indeed as if to own his debt, Virgil here adds allusions to other plays. Dido in her despair grows distracted—[74]

EURIPIDES AND HIS INFLUENCE

"*As the mad Pentheus, seeing the Maenads throng,*
Seeing the sun doubled, twinned the towers of Thebes;
Or like Orestes, Agamemnon's son,
Whom o'er the stage his mother's wraith pursues
Whirling her firebrand, with black serpents armed,
While on the threshold Fiends Avenging sit."
(IV. 469 ff.)

In Horace there is less of importance for our purpose—a few allusions in the *Odes* to Euripidean stories, a few borrowings of well-worn commonplaces, collected and exaggerated by German erudition; in the *Satires* he takes Orestes and Agave for typical instances of insanity and in the *Epistles* (I. 16. 76 ff.) he finely paraphrases the disguised Dionysus' defiance of Pentheus in *The Bacchants*, adding his own allegorical interpretation of it all: [75]

"*'Chained and manacled*
In a grim gaoler's charge thou shalt be kept.'—
'God, when I wish, will free me'.
This, I hold,
His meaning—'I shall die.' Death's the one goal
That ends life's race for ever."

THE INFLUENCE OF EURIPIDES

But Euripides' greatest debtor among the Augustans is Ovid. The least Roman of all the Latin poets, he had the Greek's gift for subtle rhetoric and psychology, though not his seriousness or sincerity. Ovid's famous *Medea* has perished; but even throughout his non-dramatic poems he adopts phrases, characters, whole stories, sometimes so happily that the world has forgotten the original. Thus his rendering of the cry of Medea:

> video meliora proboque,
> Deteriora sequor (*Metam.*, VII. 20–1)

has quite supplanted the Greek as a familiar quotation. Again those two kinds of arrows that have remained for so many centuries an indispensable part of Love's armoury come no doubt from Ovid's *Metamorphoses* (I. 468 ff.), though Ovid probably took the idea from the lines in a chorus of the *Iphigenia in Aulis:* (549 ff.)

> *"Two bows Love, the golden boy,*
> *Wields at will to ban or bless;*
> *From one he wingeth a fate of joy,*
> *From one a life's unhappiness."*

EURIPIDES AND HIS INFLUENCE

Again and again in his unveiling of the tragedies that the passions enact in the secret theatre of the heart, the Roman goes back to Euripides. Byblis' gestures in her agony of hesitation as she writes the letter that declares her guilty passion for her brother, are the gestures of Agamemnon as he writes the letter that will turn Iphigenia back from Aulis;[76] Myrrha's passion for her father follows the course of Phaedra's for her stepson, and the confession of it is wrung in the same way by her nurse from her reluctant shame.[77] Most important historically, however, is Ovid's masterly retelling of tales from Euripides. Not only do Medea, Phaedra, Andromache, and Canace appear among the heroines whose imaginary amanuensis he makes himself in the *Heroides,* but he retells at length the stories of the *Hecuba,*[78] *The Bacchants,*[79] the *Hippolytus* (twice),[80] and the *Iphigenia in Tauris,*[81] to say nothing of the lost *Phaëthon, Andromeda* and others. These versions, though of course far freer and airier and more original, may be compared with Lamb's *Tales from Shakespeare;* like Shakespeare, Euripides had not invented his stories, but, like Shakespeare, he had often stamped on them their definitive

[70]

form for ever; and in their Latin shape they constitute an important part of that buried treasure of ancient legend which Ovid was the great means of restoring to the later Middle Ages, to Boccaccio and Ariosto, Chaucer and Gower.

We have reached the point where the splendour of the ancient world begins to pale; through the long afternoon and dusk of paganism Euripides holds no less a place in the minds of lettered men; but the minds grow narrower and more barren.

Thus there is evidence that tragedy continued to be acted down to the eve of the Middle Ages, at all events in the eastern half of the empire; even in far western Morocco we hear of the *Hypsipyle* being played in the first century A.D.; [82] and performances, though often, and perhaps always, only of selected passages of dialogue without any chorus, are mentioned by Dion and Polyaenus in the second, Philostratus in the third, Synesius [83] in the fifth and Choricius in the sixth century, though Libanius in the fourth speaks of tragedy being driven from stage to schoolroom by the pantomime. This fate had overtaken it far earlier in Rome itself. The motley populace of the capital preferred the amphitheatre, and even its intellectuals the pantomime; tragedy was written only in the shape of chamber-dramas to be recited or read. Pantomime had begun with two famous masters in the reign of Augustus and consisted of a libretto sung by a chorus, while a single dancer, the real centre of attraction, maintained an accompaniment of appropriate gesture, which, it is clear, lacked neither vigour nor realism. For of one dancer of fame it is related that playing the part of the mad Hercules, he shot his arrows right into the middle of the audience and even, in a command performance, at the emperor himself;[84] another, playing the blinded Œdipus, was annihilated by the shouted scorn of a rival among the spectators—"You can *see!*" It may seem a ridiculous convention; but it is certain that the technical skill and subtlety, whatever the artistic value, and the emotional effect on the audience reached an extraordinary pitch; our nearest counterpart must be, with all its differences, the Russian Ballet. Tragic themes proved more successful than comic; accordingly pantomime not only killed, but plundered, tragedy; and once more, in the choice of such subjects as *Hercules Mad*,

THE INFLUENCE OF EURIPIDES

Agave, Ion, Pasiphaë, Telephus, The Trojan Women, reappears the dominant influence of Euripides. An interesting epigram of the *Anthology* [85] records the accomplishments of one of these pantomimic dancers in the various parts of *The Bacchants:*

"It *was Bacchus' self we saw there, when the old man led the chorus*
  Of Maenads dancing, frantic with youth and ecstasy,
And old Cadmus feebly jigging to the life he brought before us,
  And the spy that told the revels beneath the greenwood tree,
And Agāve red with slaughter of her son, exultant, mad—
  Ah, what a man he was, what a godlike gift he had!"

Again, there were those musical recitals, for which Nero had such a passion, of scenes either taken from old tragedies or specially composed, sometimes in Greek, for the purpose; and here too of the parts which we know him to have played, Canace, Hercules Mad, Orestes, Alcmaeon, and Œdipus, two are certainly, two possibly, Euripidean.[86]

EURIPIDES AND HIS INFLUENCE

But vastly more significant than these for the history of drama are the literary plays which bear the name of Seneca. We have the names of many similar writers of tragedies for recitation and a few titles of their works, which witness to the extraordinary fascination of the subject of Medea—used by Pomponius Macer the librarian of Augustus, Ovid, Seneca, Lucan, Maternus and, as late as 200 A.D., by Hosidius Geta who, according to the horrible taste of the period, made a Virgilian cento of it. But only Seneca's works have survived, destined by an accident, certainly not by their merits, to be the rock on which the drama of the Renaissance was built in Italy, France, England, and Germany. And Seneca derived so much from Euripides that he must detain us a moment here; for of the genuine plays, probably eight in number, five are Euripidean,— *Medea, Phaedra, Phoenissae, Troades, Hercules Mad*. They are melodrama of a crudity that needs reading to be believed; yet in them the playwrights of the new age found their five-act structure with something of the classical sense of form; a reflection, however distorted, of the passion and the cleverness of Euripides; the ghosts of the ancient Hades,

THE INFLUENCE OF EURIPIDES

and the ancient sense of Nemesis and Destiny.

Of the influence of Euripides on the non-dramatic Latin literature of the Empire not much need be said. It matters little that Phaedrus the fabulist (IV. 7) has translated the opening passage of the *Medea*[87] or that Statius wrote a pantomine-libretto on Agave and used Euripides for his *Thebais*—that epic, which eighteenth-century ladies took with them to Bath, none but the scholar reads today. Quintilian (X. 1. 67), while discreetly refusing to commit himself as to the rival merits of Sophocles and Euripides, makes no question that the latter is the poet for the young orator to study; and in subsequent centuries his plays continue to provide erudite allusions for such old curiosity shops as Aulus Gellius and Macrobius. Lastly, considering the influence of "Dictys Cretensis" on the Middle Ages, when it and the similar forgery of "Dares Phrygius" quite replaced Homer himself, it is worth noting that this supposed diary of the siege of Troy written or translated by one L. Septimius (fourth century A.D.), while independent of Greek Tragedy as a whole, draws directly or indirectly on the *Andromache* of Euripides. Apart, too, from third-rate scribblers it is interesting to find an indication that men of action had not forgotten him,[88] in the impressive story of Cassius Dio (77. 8), how the Emperor Caracalla, the last time he dined with the historian before his assassination (217 A.D.), when he rose to go, quoted as by a kind of premonition the beginning of that familiar verse which ends five tragedies of Euripides:

*"Most well and truly, Dion, has Euripides said,
'In many a wise is the gods' will wrought,
    And much they accomplish that none foreknows:
For things deemed sure, they bring to nought,
    And things none dreamed of, they dispose.
Even such this story's close.'"*

But it is rather in the Greek literature of the Empire that traces of his working are to be sought. Under Augustus, Dionysius of Halicarnassus praises Euripides as a model of the "smooth" style; and a far greater judge, probably of the first century A.D., the author of the *Treatise on the Sublime*, criticizes the popular favourite freely. "Euripides takes infinite pains to represent tragically the passions of love and madness, and here I think him most

THE INFLUENCE OF EURIPIDES

successful, although he is not afraid to venture into all the other fields of the imagination as well. He is by no means a titanic genius, but he often forces himself, even against the grain, to become really tragic"—and there follow the classic comparison of him with Homer's lion lashing himself to fury with his own tail, and various instances of his real success (XV. 3. 4). "He is the poet," so the critic concludes of his style, "rather of happy composition than of original genius" (XL. 3). Typical on the other hand of the popular attitude of admiration is the remark of Ælian (about 130 A.D.) on the defeat of Euripides at the Dionysia by such a nonentity as Xenocles, "whoever he may have been"—"The judges were either ignorant, imbecile philistines or else they were bribed."

Among the literary posterity of Euripides, even if rather remotely related, the Greek Novelists of the third century cannot be quite forgotten. Achilles Tatius and Heliodorus had numerous ancestors as they have had innumerable descendants; but not the least among their forbears is the Euripidean New Comedy with its involved, romantic plots, its psychology, its delicate modernizing realism;

and neglected as they are to-day, still they were dear to the Renaissance, alluded to by Shakespeare, and slept over by Pantagruel on the way to the Oracle of the Holy Bottle.

The Greek moralists again, to turn in the opposite direction, find in his characters and aphorisms endless instances to point their morals. Epictetus and Marcus Aurelius in the first and second centuries, Plotinus in the third, Julian the Apostate in the fourth, quote him incessantly; Plutarch clearly knew the plays almost by heart; and Lucian, sceptic and iconoclast, wields him alike against philosopher and priest. Assailed by furious philosophers and finding his appeal to the authority of Homer vain, "Alas!" he exclaims, "my greatest hope has failed. I must take refuge with Euripides. Perhaps he will rescue me." Of his use of the dramatist against the gods one instance will suffice, from the *Zeus as Tragic Actor* (41). "When Euripides says what he really thinks, unconstrained for the moment by the needs of his plot, just hear how bold of tongue he is:

'Zeus, whoe'er Zeus may be,—for Him I know
   Only by hearsay.'"

THE INFLUENCE OF EURIPIDES

Here at least the Christians were at one with their satirist Lucian, for Fathers like Justin Martyr, Clement of Alexandria, Arnobius, and Eusebius were quick to see in the criticism of Euripides an opportunity of dividing the pagan Beelzebub against himself. Already the Apostles of the Gentiles had given a precedent for citing their great poet in the "Evil communications corrupt good manners"—(unless indeed the line be Menander's)—of *I Corinthians,* xv, 33, alluded to by Tertullian as "that verse sanctified by the Apostle." Thus Arnobius writes tauntingly (about 300 A. D.): "Can Hercules forget his anger while the *Trachinian Women* of Sophocles or the *Hercules* of Euripides continue to be acted? These books ye should long since have burned." But far the most striking use is made of Euripides by Clement (about 200 A.D.) who finds in him, as elsewhere in pagan literature, anticipations of Christian revelation; explaining this leakage of information by the ingenious supposition that, when the Sons of God in *Genesis* had commerce with the daughters of men, they divulged to their mistresses theological mysteries which these in turn transmitted to their posterity. And so when Euripides speaks of Zeus and Hades, the God of Heaven and the God of Hell, as being one, when his Hecuba cries to the Great Cause of All, Clement sees there garbled fragments of the true faith; above all he loves *The Bacchants*, for the mystic communion of the risen Dionysus is a symbol of the mystic communion of Christ. "Come," he cries,[89] "thou troubled soul, not leaning on thy thyrsus any more nor bound with wreaths of ivy . . . here stands the Mount beloved of God, not like the tragic Cithaeron; nay, on the performance of Truth it rests, a mountain that bears not wine, but is shaded with woods that are holy. And in it there revel not the sisters of Semele the lightning-smitten, the Maenads, initiate into an unclean communion of flesh, but the daughters of God, His fair lambs, uttering the high mysteries of the Word, as they gather in a chorus that is pure. Hasten, O Tiresias, believe. The night shall flee from thee, the fire shall be afraid, and Death depart. The Heavens thou shalt see, old man, though Thebes thou seest not." It is the cry of the victorious whose enemy is given into his hand. Soon was to sound in the ears of the last great pagan Caesar the last oracle of Delphic Apollo:

*"Say ye to Caesar, 'Lo! the hall divine
Is fallen, Phoebus holds no more his shrine,
His prescient laurel, his font of prophecy,—
Yea, e'en the speaking spring is dead and dry.'"*

The old gods were put to shame and silence, their worshippers had no answer left, except

"Thou hast conquered, O pale Galilaean; the world has grown grey from thy breath"

and with it grows dim the light of Euripides. In 312 A.D. Constantine was converted; in 410 Alaric entered Rome.

III. MIDDLE AGES AND RENAISSANCE

> "Paganisme immortel, es-tu mort? On le dit,
> Mais Pan tout bas s'en moque, et la Sirène en rit."
> SAINTE-BEUVE
>
> "Ma da le mitiche vette di Fiesole,
> tra le pie storie pe'vetri, roseo
> guardava Apolline: su l' altar massimo impallidiano i cerei."
> CARDUCCI

ANY chapter on Euripidean influences in the Middle Ages is in danger of resembling that in Snorri's "Iceland" on its snakes,—"there are none." There comes indeed a sunset gleam or two between the fall of Rome and the real setting in of Medieval darkness about 600. Amid the strange exotic Orientalism of the *Dionysiaca* of Nonnus,[90] the tragedy of *The Bacchants* renews its life once more in the last Greek epic; and in a Latin work of the sixth century, the *De Bellis Libycis* of Corippus, a native of Vandalized Africa, there rings a dying echo of the same play. To Carcasan the Berber the oracle of

[82]

MIDDLE AGES AND RENAISSANCE

Ammon promises, as Dionysus to Pentheus, that he shall ride through the city-streets in triumph; and once more the ironic prophecy is fulfilled by the would-be victor's severed head (vi. 169, 184.). At the same time in Gothic Italy Boethius is still quoting Euripides.

But between barbarian and priest the theatre was dead. There is no trace of acted drama after Theodoric in the West, Justinian in the East; and even mimes and dancing were proscribed by the Trullan Council of the Church in 691. In medieval Latin and Byzantine Greek the very language of the stage has perished; "τραγῳδία" has come to mean simply "song," "δρᾶμα" "novel," and "tragoedia" any serious composition with an unhappy ending such as, for example, Chaucer's *Troylus and Cryseide*. From all the eight centuries of Byzantine literature there survives nothing like the acted medieval drama of western Christendom, only a few allegorical themes, in which it is interesting to discover—and there their interest ends—the meeting-place of the Classics with the Middle Ages, of Greek Tragedy with Mystery and Morality Play, of Euripides with Oberammergau and *Everyman*.

Such annexation of the tragedy of Dionysus

for the God of Israel had indeed begun early. We still have large fragments of the *Exodus* of one Ezekiel [91] (about 150 B.C.), including an Euripidean prologue delivered by Moses and a rather spirited account by an Egyptian Messenger of the drowning of Pharaoh and his host in the Red Sea. In the fourth century A. D. when Julian forebade Christians to teach the Classic authors, the bishop Apollinaris had tried to circumvent the edict by turning the Scriptures into epics and tragedies after the classic models; [92] in the eighth, John of Damascus made the apocryphal Susannah the subject of an "Euripidean" play and in the ninth a certain Ignatius wrote an *Adam*, "le premier essai d'un Paradis Perdu," a rude dialogue closing with the Curse:

"Thy face with sweat bedewed,
Thou shalt eat thy bread with many toils and sorrows
Until, dust-born, to dust thou shalt return."

Most Byzantine literature is either tasteless or nauseating, dish-water or ditch-water; *Adam* belongs to the former class, but to the latter the famous *Christus Patiens*, a work of the eleventh or twelfth century. Just as the Latin

West amused itself by patching up lives of Christ, mosaic-wise, out of single lines of Virgil, so this "Passion according to Euripides" of 2640 lines is sharked up, to the extent of one line in three, from seven of his plays and, less freely, from the *Prometheus Bound* and *Agamemnon* of Æschylus and the *Cassandra* of Lycophron. One is reminded of some horrible little anchorite building himself a hovel with the noble fragments of an ancient temple-frieze. There is a chorus of Galilaean women who, except for five lines of anapaests, speak the same execrable iambics as the other characters. The play begins after the betrayal and ends after the resurrection, with free changes of scene; there are no less than five messengers, the last of whom recites a reported dialogue of more than a hundred lines between Pilate, the chief priests, and the guard from the sepulchre. The Virgin is the main figure (although Christ, John, Joseph of Arimathaea, Nicodemus, and the Magdalen all appear), and opens the play with a travesty of the prologue of the *Medea,* which is really the brightest thing in the whole work. The original

"*Ah would that Argo ne'er had winged her way
To Colchis through the blue Symplegades,*

*That ne'er in glens of Pelion had fallen
Those pines beneath the axe . . ."*

becomes—

"*Ah would the snake had never entered Eden,
That in its glens the serpent ne'er had hid!*"

For Christ's trial the trial of the *Orestes* is pillaged, for Christ on the cross, Pentheus on the fir-tree. But only a perusal of the poem itself can give an idea of its fatuous incongruity, of the farrago of associations produced when Mary speaks with the voice now of Hecuba, now of Medea, now of some other heathen heroine. The author however felt not a qualm and his epilogue concludes on a note of smirking satisfaction:

"*Here is a drama true, not wrought of lies,
Nor smeared with the dung of half-wit tales of old.*"

It is poetic justice that he should be remembered to-day merely for the sake of the precious fragments of those "half-wit tales," especially of the lost close of *The Bacchants*, which he embedded in his cento. There is not in literature a more loathsome example of a great culture in its last charnel-house decay, than the work of this miserable *crétin*.[93]

Less drivelling, though also much less Euripidean, are such counterparts of the Morality Play as the *Love in Exile* of Theodore Prodromos (about 1150) and the *Fortune and the Muses* of Michael Plochiros [94] (late twelfth century). In the former Love has been put away by Kosmos, the World, who has espoused Lovelessness instead. Meeting a Stranger, she bewails her wrongs and delivers a scholastic account of her own virtues, whereby "the ancient heavens are fresh and strong," and earth sees such comrades as Orestes and Pylades, while the pernicious influence of her rival makes men hate one another like Eteocles and Polynices. The Stranger, duly impressed, proposes marriage to the lady, who as expeditiously accepts her consoler. Another work of Prodromos, lightened by some rather silly humour, is the *Battle of the Cat and the Mice*,[95] a tragic parody no doubt intended for the schoolboy. The mice, driven to desperation, resolve a mass attack on their oppressor; their king has auspiciously dreamt that he intimidated Zeus by threatening, unless vic-

EURIPIDES AND HIS INFLUENCE

tory were granted him, to devour all the sacrificial offerings; accordingly the mice, after sacrificing sheep and oxen to the gods, advance to the assault. Messengers report progress; a chorus and the Mouse-queen lament; until unforeseen victory falls to the mice by the collapse of a rafter on top of the cat.

Such is the mild second childhood of Greek tragedy; but if the Byzantines were incapable of owing much to Euripides, at least we owe Euripides to the Byzantines. They continued to read and—the vital thing—to copy him. Even so we owe much to happy chance. Three of the plays survive in only one manuscript; and seven more including *The Bacchants* might easily have perished, since Byzantine taste confined its reading to a selection, first of nine, then of three tragedies,—the strangely chosen *Hecuba, Orestes,* and *Phoenician Women.* Outraged editors may cry to heaven at the *"Byzantina barbaries"* that has mutilated our manuscripts; and yet these exist only because through the centuries, while the hosts of East and West, Islam and Christendom, rose up and seethed round the walls of Constantine and died away, while spring-winds and suns of summer rippled and silvered the blue Bosphorus, hidden away in the dust of libraries there ever sat, owlish, blear-eyed, forgetting life, some monk, some pedant, copying out in patience thousands of verses of the true worth and depth of which he probably understood as much "as a sow in the matter of spicery." Fragments, again, of the lost plays we owe in numbers to the quotations of the Byzantine learned, from Procopius to Anna Comnena, from John Malalas [96] to Tzetzes and Eustathius. One wonders vainly what Euripides can have really meant to these strangely childish minds, reading on so industriously amid the factious, futile turbulence of the Palace, the Circus, and the Church; impotent to create or even criticize; in part despising, as Christians, the vain glories of the heathen, yet wondering in their degeneracy at the wisdom of that august antiquity and proud, as Greeks, of a heritage of culture—the departed greatness of their own race and tongue to be sure—which however marked out Byzantium amid a world of barbarians.

And now, before we turn to the threshold of the Renaissance, be it said once more that it is not so much the imitations of Euripides or another that have mattered to the world; it is the effect of Greek literature as a whole, and of Euripides as one of many, in inspiring the minds of Western Christendom with a new realization of the wonder of Man, of the magnificence of this human life, in itself, alone. It signifies little that without Greek, Trissino or Garnier or Gascoigne would never have written minor plays rather like Euripides; what does matter is that without the resurrection of the Greek spirit Marlowe and Shakespeare would never have written masterpieces quite different from Euripides. The imitators have their interest; but they are a small part of our whole debt to Greece and Rome.

Meanwhile in the medieval West, Greek, with a very few and fitful exceptions, was really a dead language—*"Graecum est: non legitur"*; and even on the Latin classics the Church frowned,—Virgil was "a fair vase full of poisonous serpents," he and Plato and Terence "beasts of philosophers"; one *might* find good in the pagan writers, but only "as the cock in the fable found a pearl in a dunghill." Still the West was alive, not, like Byzantium with its mummied culture, more death's-head than feast; so that when the classics revived in the

MIDDLE AGES AND RENAISSANCE

spring of the Renaissance, it was on a green and living stock that they were grafted.

Meanwhile, as the darkness thinned, Dante could prove his unusual learning by the mention of at least the name of Euripides among the pagan poets in Limbo (*Purg.*, 22. 106); and elsewhere by explaining how tragedy (goat-song) derives its name from being, with its unhappy ending, "as rankly unpleasant as a goat," and not altogether unaptly he quotes Seneca as an example. And after him Petrarch, the Father of the Renaissance (1304-74), longed all his life in vain to be able to read the poet whom he places next after Homer among the gathered bards of his *Tenth Eclogue,* the singer who

"*Chanted the dooms of captains and of kings,*
Yet his own doom and allotted destiny
And those grim hounds fast racing on his trail
He saw not,—kings did shave their heads for him,
Mourning that he was dead."

Happier was Cyriac of Ancona in the next century—that tireless, eccentric wanderer through the lands where Greece had been. "I go," was his phrase, "to awake the dead" and at Leucosia in Cyprus he acquired both a manuscript of Euripides and sufficient Greek to translate a life of him into Latin.

And yet even for the learned of the West Euripides was for years the subordinate of his imitator Seneca. The first regular play in modern European drama, the Latin *Ecerinis* of Mussato (1315),—its hero, the atrocious Ezzelino IV of Padua,—is in form and frightfulness purely Senecan; and this influence continued to dominate Italian tragedy for exactly two hundred years and was not really dethroned for a hundred more. Renaissance criticism, likewise, seldom questioned the superiority of the Roman to a Greek, who in the words of Daniel Caietanus, editor of the first edition of Seneca (Venice, 1483), "was the son of a greengrocer and wrote in a loathsome, gloomy cavern."

But this preference was not mere caprice. Seneca wrote in the accessible Latin; a Spaniard living in the Roman centre of a Hellenized world, he was in some ways more cosmopolitan, or at least more Western, even than Euripides the Athenian; and thirdly his plays were filled with the cruelty and cleverness of devils, with immeasurable passions and uncontrollable rhetoric. All these endeared him to the Renaissance. Horrors in particular—*"Grand Guignol"* effects—were in the age of the Borgias an essential tragic convention. Thus Stiblinus the Euripidean commentator gave the first place among the plays to the somewhat unsatisfactory *Hecuba* because of its excellence in this respect; and Scaliger (1561) laid it down that tragedy must have, if not a horrible ending, at least *"res atroces"* in its action. From such a point of view Seneca was incomparable. Again his chorus, speaking in simple, monotonous metres and only between the acts, was far easier to imitate than that of the Greeks with its complex lyrics and its share in the dialogue. Even Erasmus, translating Euripides, complains of the irregularity and obscurity of his choric odes,—"Never in my opinion did antiquity show worse taste than in choruses of this sort." That ridiculous convention, too, of tragic dignity, which down to the Romantic Revival forbade French dramatists to call a spade a spade and made critics stop their polite ears when Racine used the word *"chien,"* was already growing up and naturally preferred the stilts of Seneca to the directness of Euripides, who is condemned, for instance, for stooping to describe the menial details of Ægisthus' sacrifice. Similarly, when a character in a Roman play of Trissino's says at his exit, that he is going to the stable to look after his horses, Cinthio (1553) stigmatizes it as "too *Greek* to be in keeping with the majesty of a Roman plot"; and elsewhere he sets the *Trojan Women* of Seneca above its Euripidean original. That Seneca's plays were not intended for the stage at all, the Renaissance neither knew nor cared; the revival of the *Phaedra* by Pomponius Laetus at Rome in 1490 was the first of countless performances; and reverence for an ancient covered all sins of dramatic technique.

Such considerations may make it a little more comprehensible how, expressing the opinion of their time, Scaliger could set Seneca on a level with the Greek dramatists and even, "for culture and polish," above Euripides, how Heywood could salute him as "the flower of all writers." Only voices in the wilderness like Heresbach (1551) judged him at his true worth as an inferior imitator; and it is not till the seventeenth century that this view wins acceptance with, for instance, Heinsius' definite

MIDDLE AGES AND RENAISSANCE

preference of the Greeks (1611) and Vossius' blunter: "Let him who will admire Seneca—he is nothing but epigrams."

Meanwhile however, though dimmed by this fog to a star of minor magnitude, Euripides had at least reappeared above the horizon. About 1495-6 was published at Florence the first printed edition, containing four plays, which was followed in 1504 by the Aldine, complete except for the *Electra*. In 1506 Nepos of Parma dedicated a Latin version of the *Hecuba* to one Tranquillus Molossus, who claimed a magnificent descent from Molossus, the son of Andromache and grandson of Achilles. And in 1515, just two centuries after Mussato's first modern tragedy, Trissino, the countryman and friend of Palladio, produced his *Sofonisba*, important as the first modern tragedy based on Euripides and Sophocles, the first regular classical tragedy in Italian instead of Latin, and the first to employ blank verse—the rhymeless Italian hendecasyllable. Sofonisba, daughter of Hasdrubal the Carthaginian and betrothed of Masinissa the East-Numidian, had been given instead to Syphax king of Western Numidia, as the price of his help against Rome.

With the help of Scipio Masinissa recaptures his lost bride, but the Roman dreading the union of his ally with a daughter of Carthage, claims her as Rome's prisoner. Then, as the one bridal-gift left for him to give, her desperate lover sends her a cup of poison which she drinks. The play begins with a Euripidean *résumé* of previous events, though turned from prologue-form into a dialogue with a confidant; it has five messengers; and it abandons the Senecan five-act structure and imitates the Euripidean handling of the chorus, as well as actual lines from him and Sophocles, especially, in the heroine's dying farewells, the last utterances of Alcestis. But neither the passionate fire nor the tears of Euripides ever descend on Trissino's offering.

His friend and imitator Ruccellai followed with an *Oreste* based on the *Iphigenia in Tauris*, but a thousand lines longer; and a third Florentine, Martelli produced a *Tullia*, printed in 1533,—a violent distortion of the Roman legend, imitating mainly the *Electra* of Sophocles but in some ways, as in the appearance of Romulus as *deus ex machina*, its Euripidean namesake. Alessandro Pazzi, again, produced a translation of the *Iphigenia in*

MIDDLE AGES AND RENAISSANCE

Tauris, dedicated to Pope Clement VII in 1524, and also of the *Cyclops;* and Bandello made a version of the *Hecuba* for Margaret of Navarre in 1539. But despite these poets and potentates the superiority of Euripides was not yet established. Giraldi Cinthio, dramatist and critic, headed a definite return to the fleshpots of Seneca, though at least the *Canace* of Sperone Speroni (about 1542) takes its plot by way of Ovid from that lost play of Euripides which dealt with the incest of Macareus and Canace, children of Aeolus the Wind-god. Speroni employed both a chorus of Winds and a prologue delivered, in his first version, by the ghost of the child as yet unborn;[97] in his second, by Venus who explains that she is bringing the tragedy about in revenge for the storm let loose by Aeolus on her son Aeneas,—a clear copy of the vindictive Aphrodite who opens the *Hippolytus.*

More important for its influence in England is Dolce's translation from a Latin version, of the *Phoenissae* and three other plays (1543-51); while as late as 1556 we find the *Medea, Electra, Hippolytus, Bacchants, Phoenissae* and *Cyclops* being rendered into Latin by Martirano, Bishop of Cosenza. The main point of these arid details is, on the one hand, the reëstablishment of Euripides as a living influence in the first half of the sixteenth century; on the other, the prolonged reluctance of the Renaissance to recognize the inferiority for its purposes of the Latin tragedian to his Greek master and of the Latin tongue to its daughter Italian.

Beyond the Alps the new influence, if slower, was to prove more fruitful. Again the way is paved by translations first into Latin, then into the vernacular, such as the Latin *Hecuba* and *Iphigenia* of Erasmus (1506), dedicated to the Archbishop of Canterbury, and the French *Medea*, *Hippolytus*, and *Alcestis* of Tissard (1507) and three more of the eternal *Hecubas*, in 1543 by Archibald Hay (Latin), in 1544 by de Baïf, and in 1550 by Bouchetel. Baïf's first four lines will serve as a specimen:

"*Des abysmes ie vien d'enfer profonds et noirs,
Des portes de la nuict et des obscurs manoirs,
Où les ombres des mors sans lumière ni jour
Par trop sont esloignez du céleste séjour.*"

Here is already the promise of the sonorous splendours of the century to follow.

MIDDLE AGES AND RENAISSANCE

The transition from this translating to original work is well seen in the four plays of the Scotch Professor at Bordeaux and one-time teacher of Mary Stuart, Buchanan, in which Montaigne acted, as he tells us, in his early teens,—two Latin versions of the *Medea* and *Alcestis,* and two Latin Biblical dramas, *Johannes Baptistes* (written, as he later confessed to the Inquisition at Lisbon, with reference to Henry the Eighth's treatment of Sir Thomas More), and *Jephthes* (1540-3). The latter is full of echoes of the analogous *Iphigenia in Aulis;* Jephthah's daughter is called Iphis, is given a mother to correspond to Euripides' Clytemnestra, and passes through the same phases of girlish terror succeeded by heroic exaltation as the Greek heroine,—so true to nature, yet criticized with such strange obtuseness by Aristotle as "inconsistent." [98] The description of her sacrifice, again, borrows from the account of Polyxena's death in the *Hecuba,* while Jephthah veils his face like Agamemnon at Aulis.

Within ten years there followed the first classical tragedy in French—Jodelle's *Cléopatre Captive,* a brilliant triumph celebrated by that frolic of his fellow-poets with the ivy-garlanded goat of Bacchus, which caused much scandal at the time and to us half recalls Pater's *Denys l'Auxerrois*. But the curse of Seneca lies heavy on it, as on the *Médée* of Jean de la Péruse in the next year; the latter though trumpeted as eclipsing Euripides, borrows little from him except the character of the Tutor and parts of the Messenger's account of the death of Jason's bride in the poisoned robe. Even Garnier, the greatest name in French tragedy of the sixteenth century, only continued to serve up the Senecan cabbage, with occasional sauce from Euripides, as in *La Troade* and *Antigone*. Whether he and the other French classical dramatists of the century did not write to be read rather than acted, is a disputed point; but at all events the French theatre was kept alive till the dawn of *le Roi Soleil*, not by such opiate works as theirs, but by the sweated labour of Alexandre Hardy. This poor relation of the Elizabethans failed indeed, where they succeeded, in the attempt to make a fruitful union of the Classicism of the Renaissance and the Romanticism of the Middle Ages; but he at least shook off the yoke of Seneca and the classical chorus, and his *Alceste* based on Euripides claims him a place here.

In Act I Eurystheus, at Juno's bidding, orders Hercules to fetch the dog Cerberus from Hell: Act II opens in the palace of the doomed Admetus, with his heart-broken parents wishing they could only die in his stead—an attitude they hastily abandon on the arrival of an oracle declaring that exactly in this way Admetus can be saved. Then Alcestis offers herself, but her husband refuses. None the less in Act III the gods have heard her prayer and she is dead; but Hercules arriving on his quest for Cerberus vows to restore her. After a somewhat burlesque Act IV in Hell, the play closes with effusive rejoicings that compare ill with the great silence of the heroine of Euripides when she comes back from her quiet grave.

Such was the rival influence of these two ancients on French Renaissance tragedy; in Germany and Holland the development is similar though slower—first translations of Seneca, then of Euripides, original plays first in Latin, then in the vernacular. But German backwardness and then the inroads of French classicism at the beginning of the eighteenth century delayed a real recognition of the greatness of Greek tragedy till the Romantic Revival. Thus in 1525 the pupils of Melanchthon, himself a translator of Euripides, performed the *Hecuba,* probably in Erasmus' Latin version,—the first revival of an ancient play in Germany. In 1555 came the native *Alcestis* of Hans Sachs. Then at the close of the century Strassburg becomes a great centre for school performances of Greek tragedies in Greek, Latin, and German, and also of adaptations like Calaminus' *Eli;* Spangenberg's *Alcestis* (1601), in which Hercules vanquished Death on the stage, and *Saul* (1606), which copied its mad scene from the *Heracles;* and Rhodius' *Joseph,* which not only, like countless other German and Dutch Renaissance plays on this subject, makes the most of the analogy between Phaedra and Potiphar's wife, but also, like the *Christus Patiens,* begins with an imitation of the prologue of the *Medea:*

Utinam tulisset nunquam in Aegyptum pedem
Josephus ille . . .
Ah would that Joseph ne'er had ta'en his way
To Egypt!

MIDDLE AGES AND RENAISSANCE

Such isolated instances only scratch the surface; yet even that suffices to show the influence of Euripides in these forgotten fields; and to do more certainly this book, perhaps human life, is not long enough. But his Latin rival, soon forgotten in England and naturalized in France, stubbornly keeps his hold, through the horrors of the Thirty Years War, on Opitz, Gryphius, and von Lohenstein, "the German Seneca."

In Holland, too, though Erasmus' translations had early introduced Euripides, Seneca is only shaken off at the beginning of the seventeenth century, with the definite judgments of critics like Heinsius and Vossius and the return to the Greek poet of Grotius,[99] Coster and the chief Dutch dramatist, Vondel (1640).

In England the Elizabethan drama with all its superiority shows little of Euripides. Our academic classical tragedy was almost purely Senecan and even translations of Euripides into English are rare. Ascham, however, about 1535 has the discrimination to prefer the Greek dramatists, speaks of Euripides and Sophocles as having become as familiar in Cambridge as Plautus used to be, and condemns contemporary tragedy with two exceptions as "not able to abyde the trew touche of Aristotle's preceptes and Euripides' examples." And as first Greek Professor at Cambridge Sir John Cheke lectured his way twice through both tragedians; while in Latin they were doubtless extensively performed at both Universities. Indeed the honest pride of William Soone declares (1575) that "if Euripides, Sophocles and Aristophanes could see the performances of their plays at Cambridge, their own Athens would seem stale in comparison." The only surviving Greek University play of the period, the Cambridge Ἰεφθάς of Christopherson [100] (about 1544), is based like the contemporary Latin *Jephthes* of Buchanan on the *Iphigenia in Aulis;* it possesses a similar sort of donnish merit, though as far as style is concerned Christopherson seems to take his Greek from every period, his metre from none.

But whereas eight plays of Seneca had been Englished by 1567, and ten by 1581, there are no corresponding translations of Euripides except Lady Lumley's *Iphigenia in Aulis* "out of the Greake," another *Iphigenia* in English by Peele, which two Oxford Latin epigrams record as having been successfully acted, and

MIDDLE AGES AND RENAISSANCE

a translation by Gascoigne and Kinwelmersh of Dolce's *Giocasta,* which was itself a translation of a Latin translation of the *Phoenician Women.* Gascoigne's play was acted in Gray's Inn in 1566, five years after *Gorboduc* (the first regular English tragedy in blank verse), with the addition between acts of those allegorical dumb-shows so dear to the time— Sesostris of Egypt, like Tamburlaine, in a chariot drawn by kings, a flaming grave, Curtius leaping into the chasm, the combat of Horatii and Curiatii, and lastly Fortune, likewise in a chariot drawn by "iiii noble personages."

While the educated were improving themselves with these imperfectly naturalized *remaniements* of the classics, the populace was being entertained with still more imperfectly classicized Interludes, one of which—John Pickeryng's *Horestes* of 1567 (with the H perhaps added to familiarize the name)—is another curious Euripidean relic.[101] Here the heroic figures of classic legend jostle the allegorical abstractions of the medieval Morality —Nature, Dewty, Revenge; and the tale of Pelops' line is mixed up with the horseplay of the Vice, who has displaced Electra, and the mutual head-breakings of country clowns who "fyghte at bofites with fists." Idumeus, King of Crete, who instead of Pylades is the faithful friend, quotes Plato and Socrates, and Horestes, not to be outdone, Pythagoras and Juvenal, while Clytemnestra implores her son not to repeat the matricide of Nero. Above all the author believed in action; Mycenae is stormed and Ægisthus defeated in open field before our eyes; "make your lively battel," runs the stage-direction, "and let it be long."

> *"The droum and flute play loustely,*
> *The troumpet blose a mayne,*
> *And ventrous knightes corragiously*
> *Do march before thear trayne.*
> *With speare in reste so lyvely dreste,*
> *In armour bryghte and gaye,*
> *With hey trim and trixey to*
> *Thear banners they dysplaye."*

Here is at least energy. The chief source is probably Euripides, both as being more familiar than his rivals and because Horestes is upbraided by his kinsman and wedded to Hermione, as in the *Orestes*. Crude, naïve, and hearty, this interlude is not only of interest as a relic of Euripides and forerunner of

MIDDLE AGES AND RENAISSANCE

Tamburlaine, but also as a contemporary comment, probably, on Mary Stuart and her supposed complicity, like Clytemnestra's, in her husband's murder.

But, on the whole, Euripides' individual influence on the Elizabethans, except vicariously through Seneca, remains slight. Alois Brandl suggests that the model of the *Alcestis* may have helped the supersession of Plautine plays like the *Comedy of Errors,* by Romantic drama like the *Winter's Tale;* but evidence is lacking. Churton Collins [102] went much further and, arguing that four Latin translations of all Euripides, as well as others of selected plays, had appeared between 1546 and 1597, found a number of supposed borrowings in Shakespeare. Thus he derives from Caesar's favourite lines of the *Phoenissae* (524–5) already quoted, *Henry VI* (3), 1, 2, 16,

"*But for a kingdom any oath may be broken;*"

and he parallels for instance *Richard II,* I, 3, 275-6,

"*All places that the eye of heaven visits
Are to a wise man ports and happy havens,*"

with *Fr.* 1047,

"*To the noble heart the whole, wide earth is home;*"

and *Henry IV* (1), V, 4, 121,

"*The better part of valour is discretion,*"

with *Suppl.* 510,

"*This too is valour—wise farsightedness.*"

Similarly he points out that both poets speak of "the foot of Time," that Cordelia watches over the sleeping Lear as Electra over the sleeping Orestes, that both Hermione and Katherine of Aragon speak of themselves as "shipwreck'd," that both Alcestis and Katherine at their death pray that their children may be looked after, say good-bye to their servants, bless their husbands, and ask for a fine funeral. In fact there is an M in Monmouth and Macedon and a B in both; of such criticism Tennyson justly growled that it proved plagiarism by chapter and verse if one said the sea "roared."

Perhaps the least improbable of all these parallels is that between Eteocles' speech in *Phoenissae* 504-6:

MIDDLE AGES AND RENAISSANCE

*"I'd go where rise the stars that shine in Heaven
Or under earth, could I do this and win
Fair Sovranty, the greatest of all gods,"*

and Hotspur's in *Henry IV* (1), I, 3, 201-5,

*"By heaven, methinks it were an easy leap
To pluck bright honour from the pale-fac'd moon,
Or dive into the bottom of the deep,
Where fathom-line could never touch the ground,
And pluck up drownèd Honour by the locks."*

But even here, apart from quite possible coincidence, it has been pointed out that Shakespeare is not proved a reader of Euripides, since he might have met with the passage in Gascoigne's *Giocasta* or in a translation of Plutarch's *On brotherly Love*, where it is quoted. As for the "mobled queen" of *Hamlet* she comes from Seneca by way of Marlowe. Far the most truly Euripidean thing in Shakespeare is the biting realism of *Troilus and Cressida*, where the fabled splendour of the heroes of Romance turns in hard daylight to meanness, and lechery, as fairy gold to withered leaves. But this is only the coincidence of great minds in disillusion. Shakespeare and the whole Renaissance we owe to Greece and Rome: that is surely gift enough: minor debts to this Greek and that Roman, even when they can be proved, matter little in comparison.[103]

There remains by way of contrast a later Elizabethan play avowedly based on "great Eurypedes," though quite worthless in itself,— the *Orestes* of T. Goffe, a clergyman who died in 1629, brought to the grave, it is said, by having married his predecessor's widow, who had captured him by pretending to be captivated by his sermons. Acted at Christ Church, Oxford, about 1616–20, just half a century after its namesake by Pickeryng, it is the queerest hotch-potch of Euripides and Hamlet, Pylades and Horatio, Canidia and the witches of Horace and their sisters from *Macbeth;* add some distant thunder from Æschylus, Senecan horrors, the stage-tempests of Marlowe, powder freely with Shakespearean phrase, and some conception may be formed of Goffe's farrago. His play begins with Agamemnon's murder, Clytemnestra swooning in the best manner of Lady Macbeth at the discovery, while Cassandra comes in raving, as in *Troilus and Cressida*. Orestes, who is full-grown, has recourse to the witch Canidia to identify the murderers and does "poor Yorick" over his father's skull. The horrid truth disclosed, the two comrades return to court, disguised as physician and friend, and there kill a Polonius who overhears them; next comes a scene from the *Iphigenia in Tauris* in which each pleads to be executed in the other's place. Both however are pardoned; then Ægisthus and Clytemnestra appear "in their night-robes" to take physic from the supposed doctor; and thus trapped, after their baby has been killed before them and Orestes has pulled his father's bones "from his pocket" to reproach his mother, the guilty pair are despatched. The play ends with Electra stabbing herself and the two friends hurling themselves on each other's rapiers. Parody as it is, there is a certain interest in this early tribute of imitation paid to Shakespeare so soon after his death, as well as to Euripides.

Jonson, with all his Greek learning, owed far more to Seneca in his tragedies, although he makes two or three allusions to Euripides in *Timber*. He has a fellow-feeling for the ancient's retort to the poet who jeered at him for taking three days to write as many verses, whereas he could have written a hundred himself in the time,—"Yes, and yours will not last three days, mine for all time." "I have met many of these rattles," purrs Jonson in pleased comment, "that made a noise and buzzed." "Euripides is sometimes peccant, as he is most times perfect," is his final judgment, and it is clear that Sophocles answered better to his ideal of perfection.

Not Shakespeare indeed, nor Jonson, but Milton is the first great English poet to sit at the feet of Euripides. His copy of the tragedies, bought in 1634, the year of *Comus*, with his marginal comments, exists in the British Museum. Barnes refers to these notes in his *Euripides* of 1694 and an emendation of Milton's still holds its place in the text of the *Bacchae*. Even after his sight failed, his favourite classics, according to the account given years later by a daughter who used to read to him, remained Homer, Ovid's *Metamorphoses*, and Euripides. The traces in his prose works are more obvious and less interesting. Verses of the *Medea* on freedom of thought and of *The Suppliants* on freedom of speech are prefixed to *Tetrachordon* and *Areopagitica*, while in the *Defence of the Eng-*

lish People and the *Treatise on Christian Doctrine* he finds in the latter play support both for popular liberties and for his own view of the state after death. In *Comus* (297 ff.) the Shepherd's story of the two young men he saw and thought divine, recalls the *Iphigenia in Tauris* (267 ff.), where the herdsman describes the appearance of Orestes and Pylades, mistaken for gods of the sea. Of the *Sonnets* the eighth contains a famous allusion to the tale already told—how *"the repeated air*

Of sad Electra's poet had the power
To save the Athenian walls from ruin bare."

In the twenty-third the stricken old man goes dreaming back to the happiest of the plays:

"Methought I saw my late espoused saint
    Brought to me like Alcestis from the grave,
    Whom Jove's great son to her glad husband
        gave,
    Rescued from Death by force, though pale
        and faint.

. . . .

Her face was veiled yet to my fancied sight
Love, sweetness, goodness, in her person
    shined

EURIPIDES AND HIS INFLUENCE

So clear, as in no face with more delight.
  But oh! as to embrace me she inclined,
  I waked, she fled, and day brought back my night."

Her face was veiled like that of the returning Alcestis, but in a sadder sense, for the blind poet had never seen it.

Paradise Lost,[104] also, in the tragic form originally designed for it, was to have opened with a Euripidean prologue, a cry to the Sun like Jocasta's at the beginning of the *Phoenician Women:*

"O *thou that cleav'st thy course through heaven's stars,*
Standing upon thy gold-compacted car,
With wheels of flame and flying feet of steeds,
O *Sun, how evil dawned thy light that day. . . ."*

It still survives embodied in the opening lines of Book IV,—Satan's famous address to the Sun:

"O *thou that with surpassing glory crowned,*
  Look'st from thy sole dominion like the god
  Of this new world, at whose sight all the stars
  Hide their diminished heads, to thee I call,

[114]

> *But with no friendly voice, and add thy name,*
> *O Sun, to tell thee how I hate thy beams. . . ."*

It is such instances as this of loans from one great mind to another, blessing both him that gives and him that takes, that redeem, if anything can, the too often niggardly and pettifogging study of "influences."

Elsewhere in the epic, apart from possible verbal reminiscences of the *Alcestis* and *Troades*, there is a characteristic echo of a famous utterance of Hippolytus,—a person much more like Milton than Euripides. The protest of the Amazon's son:

> "O God, why didst Thou ever set on earth
> Woman, to curse and cozen all mankind!"
> (*Hippol.*, 616 ff.)

and his regret that the race could not have been perpetuated without mothers, are repeated by the fallen Adam:

> "Oh! why did God,
> *Creator wise, that peopled highest Heaven*
> *With spirits masculine, create at last*
> *This novelty on earth, this fair defect*
> *Of Nature, and not fill the world at once*
> *With men as angels without feminine,*

*Or find some other way to generate
Mankind?"* (*P. L.,* X. 888 ff.)

Circumstances and a vein of hardness in him had qualified Milton but too well to write *con amore* on this loveless theme; and his misogyny finds yet more scope and use for Euripides' precedent in *Samson Agonistes* [105] with its Dalila, especially in the chorus that follows her repulse. Euripidean the play is in other ways too, not only in occasional borrowings of phrase, but in its sententiousness, its rhetorical debates, its lyric monodies; its very existence is justified in the preface by the precedent of St. Paul's quotation from the tragedian. Landor has accused Milton's fondness for Euripides of making him didactic where action was needed. *Samson* is no doubt rather deficient in this respect. But Euripides' plays have on the whole more, not less, action than his rivals'; and the form of *Samson*—a series of interviews—is actually closest to the *Prometheus* of Æschylus.

As for Macaulay's comparison of Milton in his fondness for his master to "the beautiful Queen of Fairyland kissing the long ears of Bottom," [106] it would need no comment, even had not its author himself recanted in his less jaunty middle-age. Meanwhile in England, before Milton died, earlier still in France, the sensitive, creative youth of the Renaissance had given place to the sensible, critical middle-age of the Neo-classic period, with a new attitude to Euripides.

IV. THE NEO-CLASSIC AGE

> "Learn hence of ancient rules a just esteem,
> To copy nature is to copy them."
> POPE
>
> " 'Monsieur, combien avez-vous de pièces de théâtre en France?' dit Candide à l'abbé; lequel répondit: 'Cinq ou six mille.' 'C'est beaucoup,' dit Candide: 'combien y en a-t-il de bonnes?' 'Quinze ou seize,' répondit l'autre. 'C'est beaucoup,' dit Martin."
> VOLTAIRE

A NEW era has begun. In the influence of the Classics on Modern Europe there are two phases; just as in Hellenism itself there were two gods, two elements. On the Middle Ages the classicism of the Renaissance bursts like the risen Dionysus,—a sudden splendour, liberating, intoxicant with the new vision of the human mind, the new beauty of the human form. But "beauty without extravagance" had been the Hellenism of Pericles; behind Dionysus treads the Dorian Apollo; and the Neo-Classicism of the seventeenth and eighteenth centuries becomes the gospel, not now of liberation but of restraint,

THE NEO-CLASSIC AGE

not of humanism but of the self-knowledge of human limitation, not of ecstasy but of sense. It is the age not of the Sistine Chapel but of Versailles, not of Rabelais but of Racine, not of Lionardo but of "one Boileau." And yet with all their meticulous worship of ancient rules, their austere refusal to recognize in Nature anything that the ancients had not seen, the neo-classics were farther from the spirit of a poet like Euripides than many who have had his name far less upon their lips. "What do they know of Plato, that only Plato know?" We shall find these prim years crowded with endless refurbishings of his plays. But what knows Phèdre of Phaedra's yearning for the wind's moan in the mountain pine-tops or the virgin meadows of the hills? When did Dionysus shout to his racing Maenads across the trim parterres of Marly in the dawn? Dramatists by the generation might learn from Euripides; but could any in that age have felt with him, it would not have been Racine its laureate, but its rebel Rousseau.

Between all French imitations of Euripides for two centuries and their original, two conventions, be it said at starting, fix an impassable gulf—the convention of *galanterie* and that of tragic dignity. Every play must contain a love intrigue; and no play must contain any person or thing remotely associated with the lower classes. "To bring," says Johnson,[107] "a lover, a lady and a rival into the fable; to entangle them in contradictory obligations, perplex them with oppositions of interest, and harass them with violence of desires inconsistent with each other; to make them meet in rapture and part in agony; to fill their mouths with hyperbolical joy and outrageous sorrow; to distress them as nothing human ever was distressed; to deliver them as nothing human ever was delivered; is the business of a modern dramatist. For this, probability is violated, life is misrepresented, and language is depraved." The slave-nurse of Euripides becomes a duenna, some Nérine or Oenone, of most respectable connections; the herdsman-messenger of the *Iphigenia in Tauris* is exalted into a prince of the blood royal of the Crimea, with a galaxy of ministers of state; and the broom of Ion the young temple-sweeper is decently huddled out of the way. Racine was criticized for degrading imperial dignity by making his Nero hide behind the arras; and his indecent use of the word *"chien,"* already mentioned, a later poet avoided by the ingenious periphrasis—"De la fidélité le respectable appui." It needed a master indeed to produce masterpieces under such conditions as these; and when produced they are magnificent, but not Euripides.

Of Corneille, romantic, *manqué* and classic only against the grain, only *Médée* (1635), his first regular tragedy, concerns us; it is still largely Senecan and its crudities were much bemocked by Voltaire from the vantage of a "correcter" age. Certainly Corneille's improvements on Euripides are not happy. Thus in the Greek, Medea sends her rival Creusa a poisoned robe; but the French Créuse is, on the contrary, so fascinated by the dress Médée is wearing that she coaxes the naturally embarrassed Jason to go and beg for her the very clothes off his wife's back. Next when the coveted robe does arrive, Jason's confidant Pollux, a suspicious person, suggests that it may have been poisoned, and accordingly it is tested on the *corpus vile* of an unhappy female, who conveniently chances to be awaiting execution in the royal dungeons. However Médée's poisons are too subtle to be so easily circumvented and refuse to attack any but Créuse and her father; next, when the messenger of the catastrophe arrives, the enchantress roots him to the ground with a magic wand, until he has told her all. At the end Créon stabs himself and Créuse dies of the poison on the stage; Médée kills her children and, after fifty lines of solitary lamentation, Jason too lays hands on himself. The Ægeus of Euripides is neatly employed to complete the essential double triangle of amorous intrigue, as the senile rival of Jason for Créuse's hand. There is scant promise in such puerilities as these of the greatness of *Le Cid* in the very next year; two lines only of the play have grown famous:

NÉRINE: *Dans un si grand revers que vous reste-t-il?*
MÉDÉE: *Moi, Moi, dis-je, et c'est assez.*

And even these are Seneca's. Euripides indeed had little for the Roman strength of Corneille; his lessons were for a younger and subtler genius.

In 1664 appeared *Les Frères Ennemis* of Racine. He had been given a thorough classical education at Port Royal; and he has left, like Milton, a copy of Euripides with his own marginalia—"Horrible!"—"Repentir trop

THE NEO-CLASSIC AGE

prompt."—"Ceçi est fort beau."—and the like; so it was natural enough that he should begin with a Euripidean plot. *Les Frères Ennemis* is based on the *Phoenissae,* though it shows also the influence of Corneille and of Rotrou, who had likewise drawn on Euripides in his *Antigone* (1638) and *Iphigénie* (1640). Corneille's judgment that the young author was no dramatist was pardonable, even if Racine never pardoned it. The way in which old Créon, the villain of the piece, spins by himself the web of intrigue which brings to destruction both the brothers and their mother Jocaste, his own son, his son's love and himself, leaving at the close a stage neatly emptied of every living thing, is more ingenious than satisfying.

Andromaque (1667) is another matter; but, as its author points out, it owes little to its Greek namesake except the general situation and the character of Hermione, the jealous wife. The simple *tendresse* of Euripides' play, one of his less striking works, has little in common with this tremendous conflict between three maniacal passions and the heroic duplicity of a mother playing coquette to save her child's life.

Iphigénie en Aulide (1674) is much closer

to the original—a perfect example of a neo-classic adaptation. Racine's audience would have been outraged at an amiable heroine being slaughtered like a sheep; and they would have laughed at the divine jugglery which substituted a hind at the last moment. The only expedient was to invent a double—*une Sosie*—sufficiently unattractive to be brought to a bad end without exciting sympathy. Enter therefore Ériphile, natural daughter of Helen and a very unpleasant young woman, her real name being likewise Iphigénie. Again, a French audience would find Ménélas *"le cocu"* slightly ludicrous; so he is expunged. But there must be some *advocatus diaboli* in his place to clamour for the sacrifice; who but Ulysse? Further there must be *galanterie;* so Achille is made in love with Iphigénie, Ériphile with him; and her jealous plot to destroy her kindly rival leads to the discovery of her own true name and her destruction. Thus the conventions are delicately and logically safeguarded; the plot is complete with perfect economy of characters; and all ends well and happily. Racine's Preface is of interest for its generous praise of Euripides and its defence of his *Alcestis* against contemporary cavillings.

"Pour ce qui regarde les passions, je me suis attaché à le suivre plus exactement. J'avoue que je lui dois un bon nombre des endroits qui ont été le plus approuvés dans ma tragédie; et je l'avoue d'autant plus volontiers, que ces approbations m'ont confirmé dans l'estime et dans la vénération que j'ai toujours eues pour les ouvrages qui nous restent de l'antiquité. J'ai reconnu avec plaisir, par l'effet qu' a produit sur notre théâtre tout ce que j'ai imité ou d'Homère ou d'Euripide, que le bon sens et la raison étoient les mêmes dans tous les siécles."

Of the unfinished *Iphigénie en Tauride* only the prose sketch for Act I remains. But the inevitable lover already appears in the shape of a son of Thoas, king of the Taurians; whose generous aid was no doubt destined to provide at the close a means of escape for Iphigénie and her brother more congenial to the seventeenth century than the intervention of a Pallas Athena lowered by a crane.

There remains the masterpiece—*Phèdre* (1677), written, it is said, to demonstrate an assertion made by Racine in the *salon* of Mme. de la Fayette to the effect that an innocent soul in misfortune was less moving than a guilty one. "The low sun makes the colour," as Tennyson puts it. Here once more Racine provides new interests of love and statecraft by introducing, as in *Iphigénie*, an apocryphal young woman,—Aricie, heiress of the dynasty dethroned by Thésée. Thus Hippolyte, who as a mere misogynist might have brought a smile to the lips of that sophisticated audience, is provided with the indispensable mistress and Phèdre with the equally indispensable rival,—a rival, on the report of Thésée's death, for the throne as well. Here, as in Seneca, who followed the lost earlier version of Euripides, Phèdre woos her stepson to his face; but the lying accusation to his returned father, Racine leaves to the confidante. At the last, after the destruction of Hippolyte at his father's prayer, Phèdre poisons herself and confesses before she dies.

Gone are the Gods of Greece, the implacable Aphrodite, the mystic maiden-head of Artemis; Hippolytus, from the wild, virginal youth, the hunter of the lonely hills, has become a polite young prince, with a feathered hat and an ornamental bodyguard. Aricie is a nonentity, Thésée a nincompoop; only Phèdre remains, outstanding, alone—

THE NEO-CLASSIC AGE

"La fille de Minos et Pasiphaé."

And in the anguish of her conscience, in her visions of eternal damnation, the dark presences of new Gods fill the void places of the old. It is the tragedy of a Christian soul bound Hellward, the sister of Dante's Francesca:

*"J'ai pour aïeul le père et le maître des dieux;
Le ciel, tout l'univers est plein de mes aïeux:
Où me cacher? Fuyons dans la nuit infernale.
Mais que dis-je? mon père y tient l'urne fatale."*

It is not Euripides; but—and to some that is even better—it is the real Racine. Critic after critic has whipped up a literary bearfight between the two masterpieces; few Frenchmen can prefer Euripides, few who are not French, Racine; but there let it rest—they are different. Racine himself was generous enough—"Quand je ne lui devrois que la seule idée du caractère de Phèdre, je pourrois dire que je lui dois ce que j'ai peut-être mis de plus raisonnable sur le théâtre."

Of the contemporary *Phèdre* of Pradon, which, by the intrigues of Racine's enemies, drew full houses while its great rival was played before empty seats, it is enough to say that it adopted the invention of Aricie and differed mainly in making Phèdre only betrothed to Thésée and so almost innocent.

Racine had often thought too of writing an *Alceste;* but it was left for a contemporary, Quinault, to produce an operatic tragedy on this theme (1674). Like Hardy before him and most other adapters since, he saves the face of Admetus by making him refuse to accept his wife's sacrifice; and of course there is a love intrigue. Admetus is mortally wounded in rescuing his bride from a rival; Alcestis devotes herself to death in his stead; Hercules, also in love with her, promises Admetus that he will bring her back from the dead, on condition that he may keep her for himself; Admetus forces himself to consent and then Hercules, better than his word, brings back Alcestis to her husband. With Lully's music the piece is said to have been effective. But the quality of these Euripidean revivals is in general less significant than their amazing quantity during this period; it is easy to count fourteen plays on Alcestis alone, excluding mere translations, in French, German, Italian, and English, in the two centuries from Hardy's in 1602 to Herder's in 1802, to say nothing of

THE NEO-CLASSIC AGE

seven on Medea, eight on Iphigenia in Tauris. Alcestis indeed even became a subject for German puppet-plays, in which the heroine having killed herself is carried off by the Devil to Hell, where she appears tortured by a dozen fiends, until Hercules arrives, scatters the devils to the winds, and brings her happily back to an Admetus turned hermit. There would be little point and much tedium in an exhaustive summary of all the vagaries of neo-classic plots; but a few are worth mention as curiosities of human ingenuity and dramatic technique.

Thus Lagrange-Chancel, a feeble successor of Racine, produced both an *Alceste* and an *Oreste et Pylade,* acted in 1697; the second effects the necessary amorous permutations and combinations by introducing Thomyris, princess of Scythia in love with Thoas, king of Tauris; Thoas in love with Iphigenia; Iphigenia in love with Pylades. There follows the stock Euripidean episode of Orestes and Pylades each striving to die in the other's place; then Thoas packs off the embarrassing Thomyris to marry the king of the Massagetae; but that resourceful lady embarks Iphigenia in her place, Orestes kills Thoas, and all is well.

There is no goddess in a machine; it is all perfectly rational and perfectly silly.

Next comes the *Alceste* of the Italian Martelli (1665-1727), interesting as an anticipation in dramatic practice of Verrall's theory that Alcestis never really died. The oracle has proclaimed that another must "go to the grave" in Admetus' place; Alcestis demands poison of her doctor, but he, prudent man, gives her a sleeping-draught; so that Hercules has merely to play Fairy Prince to the Sleeping Beauty.

In 1762-4 Gluck, like Handel before him in 1727, set to music an *Alceste* and later there came an *Iphigénie en Aulide* by du Roullet, (who follows Racine to his happy ending but leaves out Ériphile and makes the goddess content with the self-devotion of the heroine) and an *Iphigénie en Tauride* by Guillard. Gluck's *Alceste*, although it has been the only one among so many rivals to hold the stage, was coldly received on the first night in Paris; *"Alceste est tombée,"* said he dismally to Rousseau. *"Oui,"* was the reply, *"mais elle est tombée du ciel!"*

This opera was followed in 1773-4 by another with libretto by Wieland, who makes hero

THE NEO-CLASSIC AGE

and heroine vie in self-sacrifice and abolishes both the rollicking humour of Hercules and the savage altercation of Admetus with his father in Euripides, while the restrained dignity of Alcestis' return is made into sentimental melodrama; after thus destroying the point of the play with his virtuous Admetus as effectually as one who should rewrite *The Egoist* with a rehabilitation of Sir Willoughby Patterne into a perfect, gentle knight, Wieland proceeded, in a series of newspaper articles, to compare himself extremely advantageously with Euripides, and thereby goaded the young Goethe to trounce him severely in *Gods, Heroes, and Wieland*.

The close of the century completes its *Alcestis*-epidemic with three more plays, by Ducis (1778), who conceived the unhappy idea of dragging in Œdipus and making him die in place of Alcestis; by Herder (1802), with Death as the medieval skeleton and a very German restoration of the heroine by "Hygieia"; and by Alfieri (1798), who tells how he was seduced by reading Euripides to break his vow to write no more tragedies and drafted the first act at a sitting, as he says in his histrionic way,—"con furore maniaco e lagrime molte." He does not mend the play by mending the manners of Admetus' father, so that this virtuous elder competes eagerly for death with Alcestis and his son.

Some years earlier (1783) Alfieri had also written a *Polinice* based on the *Phoenissae* and having, like Racine's *Les Frères Ennemis*, a spider-Creon at the centre of the whole web of intrigue. There is in it one famous *coup de théâtre;* in Act IV an interview is arranged between the two brothers and Creon persuades one to poison the cup of reconciliation, then warns the other; on the mutual discovery the mortal combat follows.

Such were the methods of eighteenth century tragedy [108] on the continent; but to follow the details, even the names, of all its *Iphigénies* and *Médées* would take an impossible time, space, and patience; and its most famous figure has little in common with Euripides, except what a philosopher who writes plays may have with a dramatist who philosophizes. The rationalism of Voltaire's *Saul* recalls the ancient; his first impulse towards tragedy he received at the age of eighteen from seeing a performance of Malézieu's trans-

THE NEO-CLASSIC AGE

lation of the *Iphigenia in Tauris;* and *Mérope* is of course founded on a lost play of Euripides. But Voltaire remained no great admirer of his work, as will appear when we come to the criticism of the period.

Far more insignificant is the classical tragedy of the contemporary English stage; no Racine, no Alfieri even, merely a list of dramatic oddities. Charles Davenant's *Circe* draws on the *Iphigenia in Tauris;* Dryden's *Troilus and Cressida* introduces the quarrelling Atridae of the other *Iphigenia.* But who remembers now the eight times revived *Phaedra and Hippolytus* of Edmund Smith, a "scholar's play," as befitted the man who wished *Paradise Lost* had been in Latin? Equipped as it was with a prologue by Addison and an epilogue by Prior, its failure when first staged (1707) provoked an indignant number (No. 18) of *The Spectator.* It owed much to Racine,[109] but the scene is laid in Crete, where Hippolytus is in love with Ismena, captive princess of Pallene. Phaedra's nurse is replaced by Lycon, a villainous politician, who persuades Theseus to execute his son. But Smith, having sufficiently murdered Euripides, spares his

Hippolytus; for Phaedra proclaims him innocent, then stabs herself, and hero and heroine are united.

ISMENA. *O killing joy!*
HIPPOLYTUS. *O Extasie of Bliss,*
   Am I possess'd at last of my Ismena?

Forgotten too are the *Hecuba* of Richard West (not Gray's friend), ruined because "a rout of Vandals in the Galleries intimidated the young actresses," and Whitehead's anti-clerical *Creusa Queen of Athens;* forgotten, though praised by Lessing, James Thomson's ingenious *réchauffé* of the *Alcestis, Edward and Eleonora,* based on the devotion of the queen of Edward I in sucking the poison from her husband's wound. The same fate has befallen Glover's *Medea,* acted at Drury Lane in 1767, in which the heroine is temporarily insane when she kills her children, while Creon is slain by the Corinthian people and the play ends "happily" with Jason renouncing his bride and begging Medea's forgiveness. Very curious also to the literary historian is that monstrous mixture of Euripides and Ossian, Delaps' *The Captives* (1786), in which the characters of the *Helen* reappear heavily dis-

THE NEO-CLASSIC AGE

guised, Menelaus as Erragon, Prince of Sora, Theoclymenus as Connal, King of Morven, the heroine as Malvina; the happy ending of Euripides is however improved into a general massacre. To all these neo-classic resuscitations of Euripides may be applied the Rev. Genest's judgment of the last-named author's *Royal Suppliants* of 1781, based on the *Heracleidae*,—"Any person who is acquainted with the original can hardly fail to be disgusted with Delaps' play." It is well to learn of the dead, but it is also important to remain alive oneself.

The criticism of Euripides during these two centuries is likewise rather wide than deep. Renaissance criticism in Italy and France especially had made Antiquity its idol; and by turning, in the theory of Aristotle, his observations of what generally was done in tragedy into ukases about what *must* be done, and by erecting the average practice of the Greek dramatists into laws of the Medes and Persians for all drama, the Scaligers and Castelvetros had whelped and fostered that Cerberus, the law of the Three Unities. In seventeenth-century France the genius of Corneille and Racine succeeded—the first *à*

EURIPIDES AND HIS INFLUENCE

contre-coeur, the second with an easy grace—in writing great drama even in this cramping strait-waistcoat of convention. And their success in outdoing the Greeks at their own supposed game, in being correcter than the models of correctness, helped the reaction against the Classical idolatry of the Renaissance to open that War of the Ancients and the Moderns [110] which for over a century continued as an intermittent epidemic, in France and also in England, to convulse poet and pedant, the literary and the learned, in angry comparisons of what could not be compared. "For who in simple language," as the infirm astrologer said to the Chinese Emperor, "can compare the tranquillizing grace of a maiden with the invigorating pleasure of a well-contested rat-fight?" The whole idea of the progress or deterioration of the human race became involved; and while Fontenelle and Lord Chesterfield argue that cabbages are at least as big as ever they were, Huet, Bishop of Avranches throws into the opposite scale the giants of *Genesis* and the beetroots of Peru, a waggon-load each. The literary battle rages mainly over the body of Homer; but Euripides is of course engaged. Thus Ra-

THE NEO-CLASSIC AGE

cine's defence of the *Alcestis* in his preface to *Iphigénie* was provoked by the disparaging criticisms of Perrault, one of the first and fieriest Moderns. Fénélon again prefers the *Hippolytus* to *Phèdre*, being, though professedly a mediator, a stout Ancient at heart. Voltaire on the contrary, though in general no believer in human progress, grew heated by controversy into such modernist hyperboles as the amazing statement that Corneille and Racine were as great an advance on Sophocles and Euripides, as they in their turn had been on Thespis. He supports his case with criticisms of the *Alcestis*, which serve only to show how very little humour great wits may have. Elsewhere, it is true, he occasionally deviates into appreciation of Euripides whom in the *Lettres sur Oedipe* he prefers to Sophocles,—indeed "il serait le plus grand des poètes s'il était né dans un temps plus éclairé. . . . Il a laissé des oeuvres qui decèlent un génie parfait malgré les imperfections de ses tragédies." And yet a little later the flibbertigibbet harks back to such assertions as that a certain passage of nine lines in Euripides' *Hippolytus*, which Racine had copied, is "le seul bel endroit de sa tragédie et même le seul raisonnable."

His perversity without his genius passed to La Harpe (*Essai sur les Tragiques Grecs*, 1778), of whose notions of criticism the following examples, also on the *Hippolytus*, will more than suffice: "Euripide," he growls, "ne s'est pas embarrassé de faire un monstre de sa Phèdre. . . . Cette indécence grossière ne serait pas tolérée sur un théâtre épuré." His voice rises to a wail of horror—"O nature, qui êtes l'âme de la tragédie, vous que les Grecs et ce même Euripide ont souvent peinte avec des traits si vrais, est-ce ainsi que vous êtes faite! Y a-t-il des femmes comme cette Phèdre?" It was only consistent that La Harpe should likewise fall foul of Euripides' great admirer and find *Paradise Lost* inferior to, of all things, *Ossian*. The trouble with the French critics of the period was that they would not read the Greek originals—such labour indeed they openly argued to be needless; and even those who could read Greek, still resolutely refused to use any historic imagination or to think in anything but modern French.

In England the warfare of Ancient and Modern was only a minor episode, soon losing itself in the celebrated controversy on the genuineness of the *Letters of Phalaris;* and since

THE NEO-CLASSIC AGE

English classical tragedy had never seriously claimed, like French, to surpass the ancient originals, English criticism could afford to be more detached and more appreciative. Dryden indeed shows something less than his usual good sense in blaming Euripides for disregarding in *The Suppliants* those unities of place and time which in his age had not yet been invented. But that was the common error of the time and enthusiastic admirers of the Ancients like Temple and Rymer, "the worst critic that ever lived," tipped the scales much further the other way. From the latter Jeremy Collier [111] was only too delighted, in the cause of morality, to learn to exalt the ancient stage at the expense of the modern. Euripides he extols, for the opposite reason to La Harpe, because Phaedra's mad passion does *not* offend virtue. "Had Shakespeare," he proceeds "secur'd this point (of modesty, that is), for his young virgin Ophelia, the play had been better contriv'd. Since he was resolved to drown the lady like a kitten, he should have set her swimming a little sooner." John Dennis, again, the foe of Pope, not only borrowed from Euripides for his unhappy tragedies, *Iphigenia in Tauris* (1699) and a fragmentary *Hypolytus,* but in his *Reflections on a Late Rhapsody* "can by no means believe William Shakespeare to be equal in merit with Sophocles or Euripides."

Lastly the great Johnson [112] is found parodying Gray's *Elegy* with a burlesque translation of a chorus of the *Medea;* he also produced a serious version of the same passage which, although the modern reader will not find it easy to distinguish from the comic one, had the distinction of being copied out, together with the original Greek,—over two hundred and twenty words in all—in a circle an inch and a half in diameter, by Porson the great Euripidean critic. And in the very different mood of a letter to Joseph Warton, when the memory of his long dead wife has roused in him a sudden rush of that tenderness, which forms a too often forgotten side of the blunt and bear-like old dictator, Johnson adds in the stoic words of Bellerophon:

οἴμοι· τί δ' οἴμοι; θνητὰ γὰρ πεπόνθαμεν.
"*Alas! Yet why alas? Man's life is thus.*"

But though Boswell records him as reading Euripides, Johnson kept his transcendent common sense for judgments, all too few, on

THE NEO-CLASSIC AGE

tne poets of his own land; and although the *Preface to Shakespeare* disposes of the Unities with a masterly reasonableness that leaves nothing to be said, the real antidote to the pedantry of Neo-classicism was to come from Germany; where criticism instead of following upon a great creative period as in England, or accompanying it as in France, heralded its birth. Lessing was indeed playwright as well as critic; but it is the critic that matters. One however of his plays may be mentioned in passing. In *Miss Sara Sampson*, a middle-class tragedy, the hero-villain Mellefont has deserted his mistress to elope with the heroine. But his old love is furiously jealous and in one of her altercations with him betrays her real original: "Sieh in mir eine neue Medea!"; true to type she poisons her rival and flees oversea, leaving Mellefont to stab himself.

But of far more interest is the *Hamburgische Dramaturgie* [113] with its great controversy over *Mérope*. The lost Euripidean *Cresphontes* had provided a plot for Maffei, whose *Mérope* with its immediate blaze of popularity stood alone among the Italian tragedy of its day, running through four editions in twelve months. Voltaire in his turn produced an improved French version, of which he was, with some justice, proud because it broke at last with the long tradition of *galanterie*. To round off this achievement he wrote both a very flattering letter to Maffei under his own name and then a violent disparagement of Maffei in a letter to himself under a *nom de guerre*. Lessing exposed this odd manoeuvre and argued the inferiority of both modern authors to Euripides; while elsewhere in the same series he gives an ingenious defence of that stumbling-block, the Euripidean prologue, in connection with the larger question: "Should a dramatist keep his audience curious and in the dark?" There can be little doubt, though Lope de Vega thought otherwise, that the loss of surprise-effects, which in any case do not survive the first time of seeing, is more than compensated by the gain of tragic irony and the power of grasping the form of the play as a whole. The "Screen Scene" in *The School for Scandal*, for instance, would be a poor thing in comparison, if the audience were as ignorant as Sir Peter Teazle, that his lady stands behind the screen. And Lessing's emphasis of this principle considerably weakened one of the loudest French criticisms of Euripides.

French criticism indeed could make a Euripidean for the nonce even of August Wilhelm Schlegel. In 1803 an *Ion* by him, not always in the best taste, had been acted under the aegis of Goethe at Weimar, although the audience stomached it so little that Goethe himself had to stand up and quiet the hissing pit; and in 1807 in the atmosphere of Paris he boldly placed *Phèdre* below the *Hippolytus*. Yet only a year later in his *Lectures on the Drama* in Vienna Schlegel proved himself as petulant a critic of Euripides as La Harpe himself. It is as if after two thousand years Aristophanes were returned to earth, having learnt nothing and forgotten a good deal. He cannot forgive the dramatist for having views of his own about religion and ethics; himself sentimentally romantic about the deities of Olympus, he complains that Euripides thought it "too vulgar a thing to believe in the gods after the simple manner of the people," mere truth—to a Schlegel, one infers,—being much too vulgar a thing to believe in. On the very next page, however, Euripides is trounced anew for the opposite offence of conforming to the ideas of the people; "for the sake of popularity" he lets the wicked go unpunished in his plays, and

by his misogyny "he plays court to the men."
The notion that popular audiences like villains
to escape is particularly good. But worst of
all is his frightful immorality, as shown in lines
like:

"*With my tongue I swore it, never with my
heart.*"

True, Hippolytus, after this natural complaint
of the oath he has been tricked into giving,
dies rather than break it. But the good
Schlegel cannot forget "the possible abuses of
its application," and he instances those two
lines on tyranny beloved of the wicked Julius
Caesar. .And then again the horrid impro-
priety of Phaedra, of Medea—a woman actually jealous of her husband (it becomes a less
curious coincidence that both Schlegel's mar-
riages were followed by speedy separations); of
Hecuba mentioning to Agamemnon the fact
that her daughter is his mistress; or of making
Clytemnestra almost a sympathetic character!
And what can one do with a dramatist who
treats his heroes as if they were typical contemporaries? In the *Alcestis*, for example, "Hercules borders on the ludicrous"; which, as
Schlegel, had he known his subject a little

better, might have realized, is exactly what a character in a tragi-comedy (the *Alcestis* is a substitute for the satyric drama which usually followed a trilogy) frequently does border on.

The strange thing is that this second-hand and second-rate clap-trap (Schlegel also made a similar attempt to decry Molière), should have been listened to and to some extent accepted in the early nineteenth century, (Froude speaks of "Euripides whom at college we were taught to despise"), while the appreciation of Schiller and still more of Goethe was forgotten.

Schiller toiled hard, at a sort of dramatic apprenticeship, in translating (1788) the *Iphigenia in Aulis,* which he ended with the sacrifice, not the deliverance, of the heroine, so as to dispense with the *dea ex machina,* and he also translated part of the *Phoenissae.* In a letter written at the time he makes this criticism: "Often the execution is such that no poet could better it; but at times his tediousness spoils my enjoyment and my labour. In reading, one can make shift with such passages; but to have to translate them and that conscientiously. . . !" In his own attempt at tragedy in the Greek choric form, *The Bride of Messina,* he underlines his indebtedness to the fratricidal feud of the *Phoenissæ* by making Isabella allude to "the Theban brethren"; and the same *motif* perhaps recurs in the strife of Elizabeth Tudor and Maria Stuart.

But the most splendid of all examples of the influence of Euripides on an individual modern mind is offered by the great name of Goethe. A play, a play within a play, a fragment of a play,—*Iphigenie, Helena* in *Faust, Elpenor,* all three were stars that in their courses reflected the light and obeyed the power of that ancient, but undying sun.

Elpenor, commenced in 1781, never got beyond its second act; it is a queer "contamination" of the plots of the *Antiope* of Euripides, his *Cresphontes,* and—of all strange mixtures—the Chinese play on which Voltaire based his *L'Orphelin de Chine.* Antiope the heroine had lost both her husband, joint king with his brother Lycus, by murder, and her infant son by kidnapping; in both cases the guilty are unknown. Then in her childless widowhood she adopted a lad in Lycus' household, to whom at first sight she felt strangely drawn. And now the day has come when, grown to manhood, he must return to the king; and in her farewell Antiope lays upon him the duty of finding and punishing the murderers of her husband. The *dénouement* would doubtless have involved the death of Lycus, the real author of both crimes, and the recognition of mother and son.

Act III of the Second Part of *Faust* begins as with a sudden clear trumpet-call out of the ancient world—Helen, back from Troy and before Menelaus' palace in Sparta, bursting into a prologue of all the bold simplicity of Euripides:

"B*ewundert viel und viel gescholten, Helena . . .*"

From the first, of course, there is much pure Goethe mixed with the Greek; and with that strange dream-passage from Homeric Lacedaemon in the vale to the dim Gothic richness of Mistra of the Franks upon its hill—(just as the path winds up there through the green and golden glory of the orange-groves to-day) —the Hellenic fades out into the romantic Medieval. But at the beginning the echoes are clear—of Menelaus' resolve in the *Troades* to take Helen home to die the death in Sparta, of the lament in the *Hecuba* (mingled with Virgil) for the last night of Troy, of the passage in the chorus of the *Helen* about the cranes soaring high in the heavens with their cloudy cry.

But the chief interest of course attaches to the *Iphigenie* (finished 1787), though here again behind the mask of the daughter of Agamemnon speaks the voice of Frau von Stein. Reading the two plays together one is struck by the greater nobility of the German, the greater grace and truth of the Greek. The realism of Euripides is content with a beauty whose quality is never strained, the beauty of a simple episode, the natural attractiveness of characters, not heroic in their stature, but merely human, even jarring sometimes with a sense of too prosaic homeliness. Goethe, as complex beside Euripides as Euripides beside Sophocles, struggles for something nobler; not the image of Artemis but his sister's purity of soul shall cleanse his Orestes; not Pallas Athena but Truth shall save Iphigenie.

"*Alle menschliche Gebrechen
Sühnet reine Menschlichkeit.*"

The lies that Iphigenia tells to King Thoas, almost with the artistic zest of an Odysseus, stick in Iphigenie's throat; she cannot deceive even

THE NEO-CLASSIC AGE

a barbarian who has been kind to her; she stakes the life of her brother, his friend, his followers on the chance that candour and frankness will soften this savage. She succeeds; she saves both honour and life; but she spoils the play.

We are meant to admire veracity victorious; the sentimentalist will; but the Greek, whose steadfast refusal to sacrifice sense to sentiment the modern world has yet to learn, would have felt a ring of falsity in this apotheosis of truth. Whatever the Washingtonian valuation of truth in terms of cherry-trees, to balance a lie to a human-sacrificing barbarian against a single life, let alone a whole ship's company, is hysteria. The answer to Iphigenie is Ibsen's Gregers Werle. Goethe himself does not face the issue squarely. Thoas is already so angry and suspicious at Orestes' entrance, that making a clean breast to him comes to seem as much sound policy as truth for truth's sake. The moralist may swell with approval of Jeanie Deans refusing to utter a falsehood even to save her sister; common sense and common humanity will join the gallery in applauding the stage-blacksmith of an acting version of the novel: "If it had been me, I'd have sworn a hole through an iron pot." *Iphigenie* is very beautiful; but Goethe's criticism sums it: *"verteufelt human"*—"devilish ideal," as one might put it. Iphigenie says greatly:

*"*Um *Gut's zu thun braucht keiner Überlegung";*

but truer Thoas' answer:

*"*Sehr viel. Denn auch dem Guten folgt das Übel."

To that there is no reply.

On the critical side the young Goethe's excoriation of Wieland has already been mentioned, and with age his admiration for Euripides only grew. He devoted himself to a reconstruction, from the large fragments published by Hermann in 1821, of the lost *Phaethon* which he describes as "unglaublich grosz gedacht," and he was similarly interested in restoring the mutilated end of *The Bacchants,* his favourite play. The "Hans Wurst" Aristophanes and "Schlegel's own little person" he dismissed very summarily. The philologists, he complains, are as much slaves of tradition as colleges of heralds; "they cavil at him because he has long been cavilled at." "All those who denied the sublime to Euripides were either poor wretches incapable of comprehending such sublimity or shameless charlatans." [114]

Right at the end of that long life, the year 1831 is full of Euripides—"this inestimable poet," as he writes to Zelter on November 23rd, after reading the *Iphigenia in Aulis*. "His great and unique talent has roused my admiration before, but what particularly struck me this time was the boundless and powerful element on which he moves. Over the scenes of Hellas and its primitive body of legends he sails and swims like a cannon-ball in a sea of quicksilver and cannot sink even if he tried. . . . I shall not lay him aside this whole winter." And in his diary of the day before appears that gloriously absurd exaggeration: "Have all the nations of the world possessed a dramatist worthy to hand him his slippers?"

Homer and Euripides alike have been lacerated and torn to pieces by the critics and defended by the poets. Sense is more than scholarship; it is a pity that the two should seem so often incompatible; but the admired of Milton and Goethe can afford a few hundred Schlegels and La Harpes.

V. THE NINETEENTH CENTURY AND AFTER

> "Thy Phaedra and thy pale Medea were
> The birth of that more subtle wisdom which
> Dawned in the world with Socrates, to bear
> Its last most precious offspring in the rich
> And genial soul of Shakespeare. And for this
> Wit blamed thee living, Dullness taunts thee dead." [115]
>
> LORD LYTTON, EURIPIDES

IT is pleasant, as one draws to a close, to feel that in the understanding of Euripides, at least, "progress" has proved no dream; not since antiquity, in some ways perhaps not even then, has it been so possible to think and feel at one with him. For this we have in part to thank the labours of scholarship, the criticism of men like Wilamowitz-Moellendorff and Gilbert Murray; but it is largely the circling of the world itself that has wheeled his star high in our heavens once more. The one world-dramatist of the eighteenth century, Goethe, was the greatest admirer of Euripides; the one world-dramatist of the nineteenth, Ibsen,[116] though no direct indebtedness is discernible, has been his greatest and closest counterpart. The real modern influence however of Euripides is to be sought less in dramatic adaptations, though abroad these still come thick and fast, than in the rediscovery, the new appreciation, of his vital modernity as poet and thinker. In the ocean of modern literature it becomes of course more impossible than ever to trace with any completeness this diffusion of ideas often "indistinct as water is in water"; and it is certainly impossible to attempt it without offering a magnificent target to that school of critics of whom it is written:

> *"For what was there each cared no jot,*
> *But all were wroth with what was not."*

Actual dramatic imitation has been almost confined to the Continent. It is enough to mention as examples the *Iphigenia in Aulis* of Levezow (1805), Platen (1827), Bicking (1862), Burghardt (1865), R. Schmidt (1867). But more must be said of the Austrian Grillparzer's Trilogy, *The Golden Fleece* (1821), which consists of a *Medea* introduced by two shorter plays on the earlier adventures of the Argonauts at Colchis; the whole being linked together by the curse which, like the Niebelungen Hoard, the Golden Fleece brings with it. Like Goethe, Grillparzer insists on his Greeks being nobler than their Greek originals; the barbarian Medea, on the other hand, and her kin are made tenfold more barbarous. The heroine indeed is half Brynhild, half Iroquois, and Jason speaks of her in the tone of a white man who has in a moment of aberration espoused a squaw. The trouble is that the poet does not succeed in creating a character at once noble enough to win our sympathy and savage enough to explain the repulsion she excites in Greece. The nurse on the other hand is savage unmixed; and Creusa, Jason's new love, a faultless, lovable Gretchen. An additional motive for Medea's murder of her children is provided by making them too, like their father, desert her for Creusa's simple charm. The gain is doubtful; but the play as a whole is a fine work, which the reader does not soon forget. It ends with a last scene between Medea and Jason, not of hate as in the Greek, but of farewell and repentance and resignation:

THE NINETEENTH CENTURY

*"Was ist der Erde Glück? Ein Schatten.
Was ist der Erde Ruhm? Ein Traum.
Du Armer, der von Schatten du geträumt!
Der Traum ist aus, allein die Nacht noch nicht."*

The later *Medeas*, of Marbach, author also of a *Hippolytus* (1858), and of G. Conrad (1871), do not reach Grillparzer's level. As a critic of some distinction, it is interesting to find the latter echoing, in contradiction to Schlegel, Goethe's enthusiasm for Euripides, particularly the "cannon-ball in quicksilver" simile already quoted. "One of the finest pieces ever written" is his comment on Megara's speech in the *Heracles Mad* (451-94); and of Polyxena's in the *Hecuba* (343-78) he exclaims, "There is a beauty in this that nothing modern equals. Alas, to be born in an age that sees it not!"

Here we may turn to France to notice the *Alceste* (1847) and *Médée* (1855) of H. Lucas and the *Médée* of Legouvé, who adopts from Grillparzer the desertion of Medea by her children, as well as by Jason.[116a] Casimir de la Vigne produced a cantata on the subject of the *Troades* and a fragmentary *Hecuba*. And those whose schooldays have familiarized them with Mérimée's *Colomba* will recognize under the disguise of a Corsican vendetta, with its savage young girl and her milder brother, the Electra and Orestes of Euripides. The most successful modern French adaptation of his work is perhaps *L'Apollonide* of Leconte de Lisle, translator of all the plays, who closely follows the *Ion* while softening some of its ancient harshness. Thus Creusa had been wooed and won, not violated, by Apollo. And though in her mad childless jealousy she plans the murder of the unknown youth adopted by her husband, yet both her hatred and Ion's anger on discovering the plot are made less ferociously savage. Lastly Xuthus is not left at the close the gull of gods and men, but Creusa herself confesses that Ion is her son.

With the present century Euripidean themes, so far from growing exhausted, seem to have become more popular than ever abroad. The greatest of the modern adapters is Hugo von Hofmannstal. His *Alkestis*, published in 1911, while it follows the story of Euripides more closely than the eighteenth century versions, is as far or farther from his realistic psychology. Admetus here becomes a kingly soul, who, so far from craving life because he cannot endure to die, only endures to live because his kingdom needs him; Heracles a superman, not laughing and shouting over the winecup, but larger than human, the wonder of the world. Admetus says to him:

> "wenn du nur den Mund auftust,
> Ist einem doch als wüchsen alle Sterne,
> Als würden alle Wasser feuerfarb,—
> So läuft ein Wind von Wundern von dir her."

This is the atmosphere of the whole piece— the introspective impressionism of a Hamlet, in the style of Æschylus. Intense passion controlled by a self-mastering reason was the Greek ideal; passion strangled by the overmastering unreason of faith, the medieval; but reason whirled by passion into dreamland seems the mood of this modern romanticism. It is fine Gothic; but in this tumultuous flow of rather too facile fine language one wishes von Hofmannstal would remember occasionally the grim maxim: "Prends l'éloquence et tords-lui le cou." The same applies to his *Elektra* [117] (1904), Sophoclean in plot, but, unlike the *Alkestis* in the realist psychology of its ragged, repressed, and raving heroine, a mixture of Euripides and Freud.

G. Renner's *Alkestis* (1911) is a piece of unsatisfactory altruism; but R. Prechtl's (1917), a play with some real poetry in it, reads almost like Euripides re-moulding his own work, as he re-moulded his predecessors', ever closer to common reality. Here, as in the Greek, Alcestis offers to die; but while she waits for the doom she has chosen, still more when the last moment comes, her nerve fails her and she cries to keep back the gift she has promised; in vain—she is borne away to the world below and, once there in the peace of death, when life is offered her again, she refuses. Existence is too bitter.

Two more plays have been added to the long posterity of the *Hippolytus*, the *Fedra* of d'Annunzio (1909) and S. Lipider's *Hippolytos* (1913), the one sensual, the other altruistic, beyond the due measure of Euripides; and this series of *remaniements* may be closed with the *Helena's Homecoming* of Verhaeren and Zweig, Wedekind's *Herakles*, and Franz Worfel's *Troades*.

In England since 1800 there has been no counterpart of this flood of Euripidean drama; his influence has been far more diffused and its history must deal largely with criticism

THE NINETEENTH CENTURY

rather than creation. Coleridge—"to begin with Zeus"—owns in his *Table Talk* to having liked Æschylus best in boyhood, Euripides in youth and middle-age, Sophocles in his latter years. But "certainly Euripides was a greater poet in the abstract than Sophocles. His choruses may be faulty as choruses, but how beautiful and affecting they are as odes and songs!" Milton, he adds, must have liked both Euripides and Ovid just because so different from himself, "as a man of sensibilty admires a lovely woman with a feeling into which jealousy or envy cannot enter." Elsewhere the tone is less laudatory—"Euripides is like a modern Frenchman, never so happy as when giving a slap at all the gods together."

But apart from the great name of Porson, who died in 1808, the England of these years has few links with Euripides. The minds of most of the Romantic Revivalists were elsewhere. Byron indeed has devoted one over-coloured stanza of *Childe Harold* (IV. 16) to the familiar tale of the effect of Euripides' poetry on the victorious Syracusans:

"When Athens' armies fell at Syracuse
And fettered thousands bore the yoke of war,

[159]

Redemption rose up in the Attic Muse,
Her voice their only ransom from afar;
See! as they chant the tragic hymn, the car
Of the o'ermastered victor stops, the reins
Fall from his hands—his idle scimitar
Starts from his belt—he rends his captive's chains,
And bids him thank the bard for freedom and his strains."

His admiration of the *Medea* inspired only a facile, unsatisfactory rendering of one chorus, less memorable even than that gay burlesque of the Nurse's prologue, which he scribbled perched on the Symplegades, at the entrance of the Bosphorus:

"*O how I wish that an embargo*
 Had kept in port the good ship Argo,
 Who still unlaunched from Grecian stocks
 Had never passed the Azure Rocks.
 But now I fear her trip will be a
 Damned business for my Miss Medea." [118]

Yet this is at least nearer the original than Campbell's (1777-1844) solemn lacerations of another chorus in the same play:

"*In the vales of placid gladness*
 Let no rueful maniac range;

[160]

*Chase afar the fiend of madness,
  Wrench the dagger from Revenge.*

  . . . .

*Didst thou roam the paths of danger
  Hymenean joys to prove?
Spare, O sanguinary stranger,
  Pledges of thy sacred love.*

  . . . .

O *stop thy lifted arm ere yet they die,
  Nor dip thy horrid hands in infant gore.*"

Indeed the only decent translation of the time is Shelley's *Cyclops*, a piece with graceful little lyrics, which has been rather absurdly overpraised by Swinburne and others. In *Adonais*, too, the eagle eye of Churton Collins has discerned in stanza 39:

"*Peace, peace! he is not dead, he doth not sleep!
  He hath awakened from the dream of life.
'Tis we who, lost in stormy visions, keep
  With phantoms an unprofitable strife. . . .*"

a reminiscence of that famous fragment of the *Polyidus* (638), so mocked by Aristophanes:

"*Who knows if life be not more truly death,
  While death seems life there in the world below?*"

EURIPIDES AND HIS INFLUENCE

It is possible; one cannot know. But we are on firmer ground with Landor, both as critic and imitator. Euripides is discussed in the *Conversations* between Milton and Marvell and between Landor and Delille; in the latter the author puts in his own mouth a classic criticism of the number and flatness of Euripidean aphorisms: "The daemon of Socrates, not always unimportunate, followed Euripides from the school to the theatre." On the other hand: "he presents more shades and peculiarities of character than all the other poets of antiquity put together," and in poetical power "on the whole" Virgil himself is not the equal of the author of the *Alcestis*. Of Landor's poems, *Menelaus and Helen at Troy* and *Iphigenia* bear clear marks of their source; the latter is a little gem of unstrained simplicity, almost too naïve at moments, but worthy of its great original in that childish plea that Calchas may have misheard the Goddess' cry for human blood:

"If my nurse, who knew
My voice so well, sometimes misunderstood,
While I was resting on her knee both arms
And hitting it to make her mind my words,

*And looking in her face and she in mine,
Might not he also hear one word amiss,
Spoken from so far off, even from Olympus?"*

We pass to the two great figures of the next generation of poets, the Jachin and Boaz of the Victorian era, Tennyson and Browning. In Tennyson the touch of Euripides is clear but slight. *Tiresias* turns on the episode of the self-devotion of Menoeceus in the *Phoenissae*; the dream in *Lucretius* of the breasts of Helen which the sword

"*Pointed itself to pierce, but sank down shamed
  At all that beauty*"

may be linked with the *Troades;* and in the *Dream of Fair Women* appear Helen and Iphigenia and Iphigenia's counterpart in Scripture, Jephthah's Daughter, who tells of the same change in herself as in the heroine of Euripides, from girlish fear to woman's heroism:

"*When the next moon was roll'd into the sky,
  Strength came to me that equalled my desire.
How beautiful a thing it was to die
  For God and for my sire.*"

EURIPIDES AND HIS INFLUENCE

But from Browning comes the fullest tribute of the century. *Artemis Prologizes* is merely, as it were, the Goddess' opening speech in an imagined sequel to the *Hippolytus*, which should deal with the hero's healing by Asklepius, and is not particularly characteristic either of Browning or of Euripides. Browning, however, becomes very much himself in *Balaustion's Adventure* (1871) and *Aristophanes' Apology* (1875), where with great skill and not a little learning most of the shreds of tradition about Euripides are patched together into a romantic setting for translations, in the first poem, of the *Alcestis,* in the second, of the *Heracles*. *Balaustion's Adventure* is the more exciting, based as it is on the story of the Caunian ship which was allowed refuge in Syracuse only because some on board could recite fresh pieces of Euripides; it ends with a suggestion of Balaustion herself for an improved *Alcestis*,[119] making Admetus, as in several of the plays already described, not a cowardly egoist, but a martyr to duty. It is strange, yet very human—this reluctance of centuries to recognize that improving Admetus, so far from improving the play, robs it of all its point as a study in the painful growth of a character.

There is more real interest, however, in *Aristophanes' Apology,* which opens in Athens the evening after the victory of that poet's *Thesmophoriazusae* and the news of Euripides' death; and it is brought to an effective close by making Balaustion's husband that nameless Phocian who saved Athens by quoting the *Electra* before the enemy leaders in council. Browning's dramatic gift for seeing two or ten points of view at once enabled him to produce some fine, because sympathetic, criticism. Yet his sympathy is never perfect with either of the poets; Browning-Balaustion can never understand that the humour of an Aristophanes or a Rabelais is broad, not for any recondite reason, but because they liked broad humour; and as for Euripides, one feels that it is the hero of the *Herakles,* not its author, that Browning really admires. To Euripides life is a chaotic tragedy; to Browning a romantic drama; and if Euripides employed the God in the Machine, it was Browning who believed in one. What did appeal to him in the Greek was the realist, the destroyer of the conventional poetic manner, the minute observer of character. It is interesting to find Euripides his one companion in the summer when he was writing *The Ring and the Book;* and there was too the memory of the enthusiasm of his wife, whose lines on "Our Euripides the human" stand on the title-page of *Balaustion.* Hackneyed as these lines have become and in need of qualification as they always were, they cannot be quite forgotten— as her other verse about him in *A Vision of Poets* had better be.

But apart from other allusions, as in *The Ring and the Book* (X. 1667-1790), in *Bishop Blougram's Apology,* and in *Pacchiarotto, Balaustion* and its companion poem are a noble repayment of any debt; all but fanatics must regret the gabble interspersed with the poetry, so unlike the simple plainness of the Greek; but if the style makes Browning's work seem at times like a wreath of prickly furze at the feet of a marble statue, still, like the furze, it is bright and fragrant with ever-blooming flowers.

Meanwhile, however, a younger poet had attempted, and a younger yet achieved, a real revival in English of the Greek dramatic form.

THE NINETEENTH CENTURY

Matthew Arnold's [120] *Merope* (1858) follows the lost Euripidean original of Maffei and Voltaire; but Arnold's own preference was for Sophocles; and the strange frigidity of his temper, cold even in its beauty, lends little human warmth to his figures, while the hobble-de-hoy jargon of his choruses is more like Anglo-Saxon than Greek:

> "Where in secret seclusion
> Sleeps Agamemnon's unhappy
> Matricidal world-famed
> Seven-cubit-statur'd son?"

Far happier is the glimpse of Cadmus and Harmonia in *Empedocles*, after the snake-change which Dionysus foretells at the end of *The Bacchants:*

"And there they say, two bright and aged snakes,
Who once were Cadmus and Harmonia,
Bask in the glens or on the warm sea-shore,—
In breathless quiet, after all their ills.
Nor do they see their country, nor the place
Where the Sphinx lived among the frowning
   hills,
Nor the unhappy palace of their race,
Nor Thebes, nor the Ismenus, any more."

Seven years after *Merope* a new voice startled the public in a very different style, with the noblest of all revivals of Greek Tragic form—*Atalanta in Calydon*. But Swinburne with his passion for Æschylus was anything but an admirer of Euripides, whom he once called "a mutilated monkey," and even in more moderate moods described as "the most tedious of dramatists" and "full of vulgarity and void of moral sense." He emphasized in conversation [121] the fact that his own *Erechtheus* was based on Æschylus, "the style most radically contrary to the 'droppings' (as our divine and dearest Mrs. Browning so aptly rather than delicately puts it) of the scenic sophist, that can be conceived. I should like to see the play of Euripides which contains five hundred consecutive lines that could be set against as many of mine." Swinburne's criticism is too often hysterical; and at all events *Atalanta* and *Erechtheus* are both on Euripidean themes and have Euripidean prologues. Several short passages of the second are translated from Euripides and it ends with an epiphany of Athena, while *Atalanta* begins with a quotation from Euripides on its title-page, recalls the *Hippolytus* at moments quite closely, and indulges in an attitude of religious defiance which has no precedent in Æschylus. When Tennyson in his congratulatory letter to the young poet complained that it was "unfair" to attack God in choruses written in the style of the Hebrew Prophets, he was exactly reproducing the grievance of the orthodox against Euripides for sacrificing the Olympians on the very altar of Dionysus. Indeed much to Swinburne's annoyance *Atalanta* was described, though quite unfairly, in the *Athenaeum* as a translation of Euripides.

Elsewhere, his lines on William Bell Scott

*"Haply—they dream not how—
Not life but death may indeed be dead,
When silence darkens the dead man's brow"*

are a good deal closer than Shelley's to the fragment quoted in connection with *Adonais*. But such minor echoes signify little; to see the difference between the two men, it is sufficient to compare the Phaedra of the ancient with her of Swinburne's fragment.[122] The younger poet is a marvellous thing of splendour and swiftness, sword and flame; but he knew little of pity and not much of the hearts of men except their passionate perversity. The Greek original is not bettered by the sadistic ferocity of:

"*The man is choice and exquisite of mouth,
Yet in the end a curse shall curdle it.*"

It is very different with the work of that other great Pre-Raphaelite,—the medieval charm and tenderness of William Morris. The Alcestis of *The Earthly Paradise*, the tragedy of Medea at the end of *Jason*, are as beautiful in their unlikeness, as Swinburne's plays in their likeness, to the utterance and atmosphere of Greece. His Pherae seems to stand no longer on its hot Thessalian hillside, but deep in the dewy green of English downs; his Alcestis goes to death unasked and no Heracles ever brings her back to her king growing grey upon his lonely throne.

Of his namesake, once so popular, now so dead, Sir Lewis Morris, it is enough to mention the Phaedra in *The Epic of Hades;* with the usual infatuation of improvers of Euripides he ruins all by making Hippolytus first return her passion and then, conscience-stricken, decide to flee the country; so that her destruction of her own lover becomes excessively odi-

THE NINETEENTH CENTURY

ous. Equally, but less deservedly, forgotten are the *Poems* of G. A. Simcox, which include a *Sacrifice of Polyxene* and a *Troades* of a quiet, Landorian effectiveness: [123]

*"They fancy death is something hard to bear,
But we know better, O Polyxene."*

Of the criticism of the mid-century a word remains to be said. The tide sets slowly but steadily in favour of Euripides once more. Fitzgerald indeed still finds Sophocles "immeasurably superior"—"how can they call Euripides τραγικώτατος?" But Macaulay [124] comes to bless where once he banned: "I can hardly account for the contempt which, at school and at college, I felt for Euripides. I own that I like him better now than Sophocles." "The *Bacchae* is a most glorious play . . . as a piece of language, it is hardly equalled in the world. And, whether it was intended to encourage or discourage fanaticism, the picture of fanatical excitement which it exhibits has never been rivalled."

Similar was the experience of his fellow-historian Froude; and *Sea Studies* tells how, on a voyage, "for six weeks Euripides became an enchanter to me." The essay is not very striking in itself, apart from the horrific suggestion that Iphigeneia is merely a corruption of Jephthahgeneia, Jephthah's daughter; but one comes to understand how after his own religious storms he found something specially sympathetic in Euripides. And in the opposite camp, Newman [125] tells how in the troublous days of 1845 he kept ever on his lips those lines paraphrased by Horace from *the Bacchants:*

*"Pentheu,
Thebarum rector, quid me perferre patique
Indignum coges?"*

Ruskin [126] again finds summed in the *Alcestis* "the central *idea* of all Greek drama"; and Walter Pater,[127] his literary heir, in his essay on *The Bacchanals of Euripides* and his imaginary sketch *The Veiled Hippolytus,* where the author, one suspects, half identifies his own boyhood with his hero's, in a dream-embodiment of his almost sensuous leaning towards ascetic beauty, has produced the finest prose ever inspired by Euripides.

Only from abroad comes one loud dissentient voice that exacts a hearing—Nietzsche's *Birth of Tragedy* (1870-1) with its denunciation of Euripides as the destroyer of Dionysian ecstasy by his artistic Socratism—"the intelligible is the beautiful"; intruding, like Anaxagoras, his "Mind" on the imaginative world of his predecessors, this intellectual might seem indeed by contrast "sober among men drunk"; but in effect he came to destroy not to fulfill the old inspiration, repenting only when it was too late, in *The Bacchants*, where the symbol of his own doom appears in Cadmus turned serpent in his subtlety. "O impious Euripides, thy very heroes have only counterfeit masked passions and speak only counterfeit masked music." Brilliant criticism, were it only true!

But when all is said, it is not the judgments of literary men upon the classics, with which their acquaintance has tended through the decay of classical education to grow less and less, but the humanization of scholarship itself that has so increased, in the last half-century, the appreciation of Euripides, as of Greek literature in general, in ways beyond the imagination of a Paley or a Barnes. The work of Wilamowitz-Moellendorff in Germany, of Patin, Decharme, and Masqueray in France, of Verrall and Gilbert Murray in England has revolutionized the sciolist generalizations of the eighteenth and early nineteenth centuries; and it is significant for the twentieth, to find the last-named under a thin disguise in Shaw's *Major Barbara*, quoting from his own translation of *The Bacchants* to a manufacturer of munitions who aptly replies with the adaptation of Plato: "Society cannot be saved until either professors of Greek take to making gunpowder or else makers of gunpowder become professors of Greek."

Indeed the defence of the Classics is not that they are venerable and mouldy antiques, the sources of modern civilization; there is little living water in "sources"; let the dead bury their dead and pedants pedants. Euripides matters to-day not as an ancient but as a modern, not because he inspired Menander and Seneca and Plutarch but because he can inspire us, not because twenty-three centuries have left him great but because for almost two millennia he has been too modern for men fully to understand. In his own lifetime worshipped by a few, by the most despised; for close on a thousand years the New Testament of Paganism, in its grandeur and its wane; for close on a thousand more, dumb to the West and mumbled only by the toothless dotage of Byzantium; then, through Seneca and in himself, one of the rocks on which the stage of modern Europe has been built, the idol of Milton and Goethe and Browning; to-day he greets us as the poet-thinker vexed by the same thoughts that our last generations know but too well. If witness is needed, it is enough to turn to the resurrection in Ibsen of the power, the passion, and the purpose of Euripides. The intense individualism, the bold questioning of all orthodox tradition, the change from the spirit of Kingsley's "Be good, sweet maid, and let who can, be clever" to that of Meredith's "More brain, O Lord, more brain!" the realization that life is too complex for rules of thumb, that from all moral codes and catchwords and taboos there lies always the appeal to common sense and common humanity—all these themes of the dramatist of modern life had already found their utterance on that stage of long ago; and to us whose days are spent in a civilization as doomed, maybe, as Greece, who have seen in our time whole peoples swallowed in the unpitied ruin of Troy, whose world has been poisoned with the blind hatred and yet blinder statecraft of modern sons of Atreus and Laertes—"the ancient, blinded vengeance and the wrong that amendeth wrong,"—to us the poet of the *Medea* and the *Troades* and the *Electra* can be no mere antique. Even were it not so, even in a happier age, he would still be "Euripides the human," great for his influence not only on the past but on the present and the future of mankind. Meanwhile for a little he is ours:

> *"Look thy last on all things lovely*
> *Every hour; let no night*
> *Seal thy sense in deathly slumber*
>   *Till to delight*
> *Thou have paid thy utmost blessing,*
> *Since that all things thou wouldst praise*
> *Beauty took from those who loved them*
>   *In other days."*

NOTES AND BIBLIOGRAPHY

NOTES

1. 480 B.C: the Parian Marble however dates his birth 485-4, perhaps correctly.
2. *Fragment* 282, in A. Nauck's *Tragicorum Graecorum Fragmenta, Leipzig,* 1889 [2].
3. Aristotle, *Poetics,* XVIII. 7.
4. Dryden, *Essay on Dramatic Poesy.*
5. Induction to *A Warning for Faire Women,* 1599.
6. *Andromeda, fr.* 132. *Cf. The Tempest* III. 1. 83–4.
    "I'll be your wife if you will marry me,
        If not, I'll die your maid."
7. Eur., *Medea,* 248–254. This and subsequent translations are the author's.
8. Plutarch, *De Superstitione,* 10. (170B).
9. *Troades,* 95–97.
10. Aristophanes, *Acharnians,* 393 ff.
11. Aristotle, *Poetics,* XXV. 6.
12. It is worth noting too that fondness for tragic child-characters (e.g. in *Medea, Heracles, Andromache,* and *Alcestis*) which marks out Euripides among ancient dramatists and joins him with Shakespeare and Maeterlinck among the moderns.
13. *Medea,* 1040 ff.
14. *Hecuba,* 409 ff.
15. Aristotle, *Poetics,* XXII. 8.
16. VII. 1. 50.
17. Aristotle records (*Rhet.,* III. 15) that this line was even brought up against Euripides as evidence of impiety by one Hygiainon, his opponent in a lawsuit.
18. Cf. the dialogue in Voltaire's *Saul,* I. 3 (very Euripidean in its method of attack):
SAMUEL. "Saul, ci-devant roi des Juifs, Dieu ne vous avait-il ordonné par ma bouche d'égorger tous les Amal-

NOTES

écites sans épargner ni les femmes ni les filles ni les enfants à la mamelle?"

AGAG. "Ton Dieu t'avait ordonné? Tu t'es trompé; tu voulais dire ton diable."

19. *Auge, fr.* 266, *Heracles*, 1341 ff.

20. *Fr.*, 286.

21. 884 ff.

22. *Heracleidae*, 593–6.

23. This might seem an instance of the fallacy of attributing to the poet the views of his characters. But Euripides harps on this theme, for its own sake, too clearly (cf. *Iphig. Aul.*, 526, *Fr.* 973) for any real doubt.

24. *Helen*, 747–8, 755–7.

25. *Electra*, 294 ff.

26. *Fr.* 1047.

27. See however *Fr.* 525, where an (eugenic) argument in favour of her manlike freedom is put into the mouth of Atalanta.

28. Lysias, *Adv. Simon.* 6, speaks, for instance, of women so respectable that they were ashamed to be seen by their own male relations.

29. *Fr.* 1036.

30. *Cf.* Aelian, *Var. Hist.*, II. 13; Diog. Laert., II. 18.

31. 868–869. Cf. Cratinus' mocking compound—"$^{h}εὐριπιδαριστοφανίζων$."

32. Schol. on Aristophanes, *Clouds* 145; Suidas, "$σοφός$."

33. Plutarch, *Nicias*, 29.

34. Diod. Sic., XIII. 97. As I write (Dec. 1922) history has just strangely repeated itself and Athens has sent to merciless execution another six of her rulers.

35. Plutarch, *Lysander*, 15.

36. *Fr.* 449.

37. Cf. also *Rep.*, 568A and B, and *Troad.*, 1169, *Protag.*, 352B, and *Hippol.*, 377ff.; and see *Gorg.*, 485E, 492E, *Theaet.*, 154D, *Sympos.*, 177A, [*Epist.* 1, 309 D.]

38. Diog. Laert., II. 78.

39. *Cf. Fr.* 841. "Alas, the very curse of God on man
   Is this—when we see right, yet do it not."

NOTES

40. Demosthenes, *De Falsa Légatione,* 245, *De Corona,* 267.

41. Aeschines, *In Timarchum,* 128, 151–2.

42. Lycurgus, *Leocrates,* 100.

43. *I. G.* II, 973; *cf.* A. Wilhelm, *Urkunden Dramatischer Aufführungen in Athen,* pp. 38–40, Wièn, 1906.

44. Plutarch, *Pelopidas,* 29.

45. Pseudo-Plut., *Lives of the Ten Orators, Isocrates,* 837E. The three lines were *Archelaus.* (*fr.* 228), 1:*Iphig. Taur.,* 1:*Phrixus,* (fr. 819), 1.

46. Plutarch, *Timoleon,* 37.

47. Plutarch, *Alexander,* 10.

48. Plutarch, *Alexander,* 8.

49. Plutarch, *Alexander,* 51; see also 53.

50. Arrian, *Exp. Alex.,* VII. 16. 6: the same line is twice quoted by Cicero.

51. Athenæus, 537 D.

52. Two quotations of Eur. in the life of Demetrius are also of interest: Plutarch, *Demetrius,* 14 and 45.

53. Diog. Laert., IV. 26.

54. Diog. Laert., IV. 29.

55. Diog. Laert., VII. 180; cf. Aul. Gell., VI. 16. 7.

56. Aul. Gell., XV. 20. 8.

57. Lucian, *How to write History,* 1.

58. *Bull. Corr. Hell.,* XVII. 84 (1894). Capps rightly dates the inscription in the third century B.C.; in *Transactions of the American Philological Association,* XXXI. 135 [1900].

59. Philostratus, *Imagines,* ii. 4.

60. G. Körte, *I Relievi delle Urne Etrusche,* Berlin, 1870–1916.

61. Ennius, *Fr.* 309 in Diehl's edition, *Poetarum Romanorum Veterum Reliquiae,* Bonn, 1911. In Roman *Comedy,* the only references known to me are Plautus, *Rudens,* I. 1. 4. "Non ventus fuit, verum Alcumena Euripidi," and Terence, *Phormio,* 241–245; cf. *Fr.* 964 of Euripides.

62. Cf. especially Lucretius, I. 94. (*Quod patrio princeps* . . .) and *I. A.,* 1220.

NOTES

63. Plutarch, *Crassus*, 33.
64. Suetonius, *Cæsar*, 30.
65. Cicero, *De Officiis*, III. 21. 82.
66. Plutarch, *Brutus*, 51.
67. Suetonius, *Augustus*, 25.
68. Cass. Dio, LVIII. 24; cf. Cicero, *Ad Att.*, II. 25.
69. *Aen.* I. 203. Cf. *Andromeda, Fr.* 133, also quoted in an amusing passage of Theophrastus (*Char.* 20), in Cic., *De Finibus*, II. 32. 105, in Seneca, *Herc. Fur.*, 656 and in several other places. It may have been suggested by Homer, *Od.*, XV. 400.
70. *Cf. Aen.*, II. 56 and *Troades*, 45; *Aen.*, II. 31–4 and *Troades* 531ff; *Aen.*, II. 325 and *Troades*, 581–2. (A clear case.)
71. *Aen.*, II. 567ff.
72. *Aen.*, VII. 761ff.
73. *Aen.*, XI. 841ff.
74. *Cf.* too *Aen.*, IV. 698 and *Alcest.*, 74ff. (the fatal tress on which the heroine's life depends; and see Servius on *Aen.*, VII. 337).

There is also a close parallel between the dialogue of the lovesick Scylla with her nurse in the doubtful *Ciris*, 220 ff. and the similar scene in the *Hippolytus*.

75. Hor., *Odes*, II. 19, III. 25, IV. 7, 25; *Epod.*, 3. 13–4; *Epist.*, I. 18. 43.
76. Ovid, *Metamorphoses*, IX. 522 ff.; *I. A.*, 36 ff.
77. *Met.*, X. 382 ff.
78. *Met.*, XIII. 440 ff.
79. *Met.*, III. 511 ff.
80. *Met.*, XV. 492 ff.; *Fasti*, VI. 737 ff..
81. *Ex Ponto*, III. 2. 43 ff. See also *Heroid.* 4 (Phaedra to Hippolytus) and 8 (Hermione to Orestes), *Trist*, II. 526, and *A. A.*, *I.* 335–6 (Medea); and *cf. Her.*, 21, 135 with *Hipp.* 612, *Fast.*, I. 493–4 with *Fr.* 1047, IV. 521 with *Hipp.* 1396; lastly, *Ibis*, 597–8 refers to the legend of Euripides' death.
82. Athenaeus, 343 E, F.
83. Dio Chrys., XIX. 487; Philostratus, *Vita Apoll.*, VII. 5; Synesius, *De provid.*, 106 A.

NOTES

84. Macrobius, II. 7. See, on the whole subject of pantomine, etc., L. Friedländer, *Roman Life and Manners*, New York and London, 1913; II. 99ff. Audiences were clearly very critical and convention very strong; cf. the story of the actor whose representation of Semele being consumed by the lightnings of Zeus was condemned as suggesting rather the (Euripidean) subject of Medea's rival being consumed by her poisoned robe.

85. *Append. Planud.*, 289; cf. 290.

86. Suetonius, *Nero*, 21 and 46. Cass. Dio, LXIX. 9, 10, and 22.

87. It is worth comparing the version of *Ennius*, (*Fr.* 306).

88. Amm. Marcell., XXVII. 4. 8, mentions the tomb of Euripides in Macedonia as still a familiar object of pilgrimage in the fourth century A.D.

89. Clem. Alex., *Protrepticus*, 119; cf. 76 (attack on Apollo and Heracles with quotations from *Orestes* and *Alcestis*), 25, and numerous other passages, especially, *Stromata*, V. p. 688 and *passim*.

90. Nonnus, *Dionys.*, XLVI.

91. Published with the *Fragments of Euripides* (Firmin-Didot, Paris, 1846).

92. Sozomen, V. 18.

93. Published in the same volume as Ezekiel above, n. 91.

94. Published in the same volume as Ezekiel above, n. 91.

95. Edited by Hercher in the *Teubner Series*, Leipzig, 1873.

96. Responsible for the curious statement that "the wise Euripides" (as he always calls him) "produced a play about the Cyclops having *three* eyes."

97. An absurdity introduced into Gay's burlesque *"The What d'ye Call It?"*

98. Aristotle, *Poetics*, XV. 5.

99. As an international jurist, Grotius brings a discussion of the famous *Hippol.* passage ("With my tongue I swore it, never with my heart") into his *De Jure Belli et Pacis*, II. 13. 2.

[183]

NOTES

100. See F. S. Boas, *University Drama in the Tudor Age*, chapter III.

101. *Horestes* is reprinted in A. Brandl's *Quellen des weltlichen Dramas in England vor Shakespeare*, Strassburg, 1898.

102. John Churton Collins, *Studies in Shakespeare*, New York, 1904, pp. 46–91, where numerous other parallels are drawn,—e. g. *All's Well that End's Well*, II. 3. 1 and *Fr.* 913; *Hamlet*, I. 5. 55–7 and *Fr. 213;* *Mid. Night's Dream*, I. 1. 234 and *Fr.* 909, 6; *Rom. and Jul.*, IV. 5. 35–6 and *I.A.*, 460–1.

103. The opening of Act I (?Shakespeare's) of *The Two Noble Kinsmen* bears a resemblance to the corresponding scene of *The Suppliants*, which *may* not be accidental. On the other hand Spencerian allusions like the fine description of Hippolytus' end in *F. Q.*, V. 8. 43 and of Medea and "the enchanted flame that did Creusa wed" in *F. Q.*, II. 12. 44 need not be traced further back than Ovid. There is a curious stray allusion in Meres' consolation to Nashe on being imprisoned for his *Isle of Dogs*—"Dogs were the death of Euripides; thine are but paper dogs."

104. *Cf.* too *Par. Lost*, V. 76 and *Alcest.*, 18.

105. Cf. *S. A.*, 549 and *The Suppliants*, 650; *S. A.*, 982 ff. and *Heracleid.*, 597 ff.

106. Macaulay, *Essay on Milton*.

107. Johnson, *Preface to Shakespeare*.

108. Of neo-classic German drama it is enough to mention the names of J. E. Schlegel (*Hecuba*, 1736, revised as *Die Trojanerinnen*, 1742, and *Geschwister in Taurien*, 1737–9: strong French influence) and von Derschau (*Orestes u. Pylades*, 1747: poor).

109. Similarly, Philips' *Distressed Mother* of 1712 was an adaptation of *Andromaque*. Of it the Rev. Genest remarks with angry scorn that the incongruous word "Madam" recurs 54 times.

110. See Bury, *The Idea of Progress*, chapters IV–V; and A. H. Rigault, *Histoire de la querelle des Anciens et des Modernes*, Paris, 1859.

NOTES

111. Jeremy Collier, *Short View of the Immortality and Profaneness of the English Stage,* London, 1696.

112. See Birkbeck Hill's *Johnsonian Miscellanies,* Oxford, 1897; I. 191.

113. *Hamb. Dram.,* Nos. 36–50.

114. *Conversations with Eckermann,* March 23, 1827 and Feb. 13, 1831.

115. The whole poem (to be found among *Early Poems,* in Vol. III of Lord Lytton's *Poetical and Dramatic Works*), though not first-rate verse, contains some excellent criticism and is worth reading through.

116. For Euripides-Ibsen parallel see H. Steiger, *Euripides,* Leipzig, 1912.

116. a. Cf., also, the *Médée* of Catulle Mendès (1898).

117. Translated by A. Symons, London, 1908.

118. There is also a paraphrase by André Chénier.

119. A fruit, perhaps, of this suggestion (at least Balaustion's words are quoted on its title page) is J. Todhunter's *Alcestis* (1879): as usual it makes Admetus ignorant of Alcestis' sacrifice until too late and as usual it spoils the final scene of her return.

120. Talfourd's frigid *Ion* of a quarter of a century before has nothing in common with Euripides' play beyond the name.

121. Gosse, *Portraits and Sketches,* "Swinburne."

122. "Phaedra," *Poems and Ballads, First Series*.

123. Similar in style is William Cory's "Phaedra's Nurse" (a rendering of *Hippol.* 176–197), in his *Ionica* (1858).

124. For Macaulay's criticisms see the Appendix to Trevelyan's *Life*.

125. John Henry Newman, *History of my Religious Opinions,* p. 294, London, 1865.

126. Ruskin, *Modern Painters,* Vol. V, Pt. ix, Chapter II, 15. The "idea" being that "At the close of a Greek tragedy there are far-off sounds of a divine triumph and a glory as of resurrection,"—which is more beautiful than true.

127. Walter Pater, *Greek Studies,* New York, 1901.

BIBLIOGRAPHY

BOAS., F. S., *University Drama in the Tudor Age*. Oxford, 1914.

CREIZENACH, WILHELM M. A., *Geschichte des neueren Dramas*. Halle a. S., 5 vols. 1893–1916.

CUNLIFFE, J. W., *Early English Classical Tragedies*. Oxford, 1912.

CUNLIFFE, J. W., *Influence of Seneca on Elizabethan Tragedy*. London and New York, 1893.

DECHARME, PAUL, *Euripide et l'esprit de son théâtre*. Paris, 1893. Translation, *Euripides and the Spirit of his Dramas*, by James Loeb. London and New York, 1906.

FLICKINGER, R. C., *The Greek Theater and Its Drama*. Chicago, 1922.

GENEST, JOHN, *Some Account of the English Stage*, from the Restoration in 1660 to 1830. Bath, 1832. For reference only.

GOODELL, T. D., *Athenian Tragedy*. New Haven, 1920.

HAIGH, A. E., *The Attic Theatre*. Oxford, 1907.

HAIGH, A. E., *The Tragic Drama of the Greeks*. Oxford, 1896.

HEINEMANN, KARL, *Die Tragischen Gestalten der Griechen in der Weltliteratur*, in the Series *Das Erbe der Alten*. 2 vols. Leipzig, 1920.
  Deals exclusively with the drama but is of much interest.

HUDDILSTON, J. H., *Greek Tragedy in the light of Vase Paintings*. London and New York, 1898.

HUDDILSTON, J. H., *The Attitude of the Greek Tragedians toward Art*. London and New York, 1898.

KRUMBACHER, KARL, *Geschichte der Byzantinischen Litteratur*. Munich, 1891.

LUCAS, F. L., *Seneca and Elizabethan Tragedy*. Cambridge, England, 1922.

BIBLIOGRAPHY

MASQUERAY, PAUL, *Euripide et Ses Idées*. Paris, 1908.

MURRAY, GILBERT, *A History of Ancient Greek Literature*, in the Series, *Literatures of the World*. London and New York, 1908.

MURRAY, GILBERT, *The Athenian Drama*. London, 1902.
Cf., especially, introduction to volume II.

MURRAY, GILBERT, *Euripides and his Age*, in the *Home University Library*. London and New York, 1913. Much the best book for the general reader.

MURRAY, GILBERT, Verse translations of: *Hippolytus, Troades, Bacchae, Medea, Iphigenia in Tauris, Electra, Rhesus*, London, 1911.

Excellent verse, but most misleadingly romantic; in fact, as much an adaption as a translation of Euripides.

NESTLE, WILHELM, *Euripides der Dichter der griechischen Aufklärung*. Stuttgart, 1901.

NORWOOD, G., *Euripides and Bernard Shaw*. London and Boston, 1921.

NORWOOD, G., *Greek Tragedy*. London, 1920.

PATIN, HENRI J. G., *Études sur les Tragiques Grecs*. Paris, 1884.

Still good, with much interesting comparison of French classical tragedies.

PETERSEN, EUGEN, *Die Attische Tragödie als Bild-und Bühnenkunst*. Bonn, 1915.

RIBBECK, O., *Römische Tragödie*. Leipzig, 1875.

SARCEY, F., *Quarante Ans de Théâtre: feuilletons dramatiques*. 8 vols. Paris, 1900–02. Contains dramatic criticism of Euripides and Racine.

SHEPPARD, J. T., *Greek Tragedy* (Cambridge Manuals). Cambridge, England, 1911.

STACKEL, PAUL, *Seneca und das deutsche Renaissancedrama*. Berlin, 1907.

STEIGER, HUGO, *Euripides: Seine Dichtung und Seine Persönlichkeit*, in the series, *Das Erbe Der Alten*. Leipzig, 1912.

VERRALL, A. W., *Essays on Four Plays of Euripides*. Cambridge, England, 1905.

BIBLIOGRAPHY

VERRALL, A. W., *Euripides, the Rationalist.* Cambridge, England, 1895.

WAY, A. S., *The Tragedies of Euripides,* in English verse. 3 vols. London and New York, 1894–8. Good, though too archaic. Also, in *The Loeb Classical Library.*

WEIL, HENRI, *Études sur le Drame antique.* Paris, 1908.

WILAMOWITZ-MOELLENDORFF, ULRICH VON, *Herakles;* cf. the introduction to the first edition. Berlin, 1889

Our Debt to Greece and Rome

AUTHORS AND TITLES

AUTHORS AND TITLES

1. HOMER. John A. Scott, *Northwestern University*.
2. SAPPHO. David M. Robinson, *The Johns Hopkins University*.
3A. EURIPIDES. F. L. Lucas, *King's College, Cambridge*.
3B. AESCHYLUS AND SOPHOCLES. J. T. Sheppard, *King's College, Cambridge*.
4. ARISTOPHANES. Louis E. Lord, *Oberlin College*.
5. DEMOSTHENES. Charles D. Adams, *Dartmouth College*.
6. ARISTOTLE'S POETICS. Lane Cooper, *Cornell University*.
7. GREEK HISTORIANS. Alfred E. Zimmern, *University of Wales*.
8. LUCIAN. Francis G. Allinson, *Brown University*.
9. PLAUTUS AND TERENCE. Charles Knapp, *Barnard College, Columbia University*.
10A. CICERO. John C. Rolfe, *University of Pennsylvania*.
10B. CICERO AS PHILOSOPHER. Nelson G. McCrea, *Columbia University*.
11. CATULLUS. Karl P. Harrington, *Wesleyan University*.
12. LUCRETIUS AND EPICUREANISM. George Depue Hadzsits, *University of Pennsylvania*.
13. OVID. Edward K. Rand, *Harvard University*.
14. HORACE. Grant Showerman, *University of Wisconsin*.
15. VIRGIL. John William Mackail, *Balliol College, Oxford*.
16. SENECA. Richard Mott Gummere, *The William Penn Charter School*.
17. ROMAN HISTORIANS. G. Ferrero, *Florence*.
18. MARTIAL. Paul Nixon, *Bowdoin College*.
19. PLATONISM. Alfred Edward Taylor, *St. Andrew's University*.
20. ARISTOTELIANISM. John L. Stocks, *St. John's College, Oxford*.
21. STOICISM. Robert Mark Wenley, *University of Michigan*.
22. LANGUAGE AND PHILOLOGY. Roland G. Kent, *University of Pennsylvania*.
23. RHETORIC AND LITERARY CRITICISM.
24. GREEK RELIGION. Walter W. Hyde, *University of Pennsylvania*.
25. ROMAN RELIGION. Gordon J. Laing, *McGill University*.

AUTHORS AND TITLES

26. MYTHOLOGIES. Jane Ellen Harrison, *Newnham College, Cambridge.*
27. THEORIES REGARDING THE IMMORTALITY OF THE SOUL. Clifford H. Moore, *Harvard University.*
28. STAGE ANTIQUITIES. James T. Allen, *University of California.*
29. GREEK POLITICS. Ernest Barker, *King's College, University of London.*
30. ROMAN POLITICS. Frank Frost Abbott, *Princeton University.*
31. ROMAN LAW. Roscoe Pound, *Harvard Law School.*
32. ECONOMICS AND SOCIETY. M. T. Rostovtzeff, *University of Wisconsin.*
33. WARFARE BY LAND AND SEA. E. S. McCartney, *University of Michigan.*
34. THE GREEK FATHERS. Roy J. Deferrari, *The Catholic University of America.*
35. BIOLOGY AND MEDICINE. Henry Osborn Taylor, *New York.*
36. MATHEMATICS. David Eugene Smith, *Teachers College, Columbia University.*
37. LOVE OF NATURE. H. R. Fairclough, *Leland Stanford Junior University.*
38. ASTRONOMY AND ASTROLOGY. Franz Cumont, *Brussels.*
39. THE FINE ARTS. Arthur Fairbanks, *Museum of Fine Arts, Boston.*
40. ARCHITECTURE. Alfred M. Brooks, *Swarthmore College.*

41. ENGINEERING. Alexander P. Gest, *Philadelphia.*
42. GREEK PRIVATE LIFE, ITS SURVIVALS. Charles Burton Gulick, *Harvard University.*
43. ROMAN PRIVATE LIFE, ITS SURVIVALS. Walton B. McDaniel, *University of Pennsylvania.*
44. FOLK LORE. Campbell Bonner, *University of Michigan.*
45. GREEK AND ROMAN EDUCATION.

46. CHRISTIAN LATIN WRITERS. Andrew F. West, *Princeton University.*
47. ROMAN POETRY AND ITS INFLUENCE UPON EUROPEAN CULTURE. Paul Shorey, *University of Chicago.*
48. PSYCHOLOGY.
49. MUSIC. Théodore Reinach, *Paris.*
50. ANCIENT AND MODERN ROME. Rodolfo Lanciani, *Rome.*